$4.9

HAN

The glorious hour
Lt. Monroe

The Glorious Hour
of Lt. Monroe

The Glorious Hour
of Lt. Monroe

by

RICHARD HANSER

ILLUSTRATED WITH

MAPS, PORTRAITS, AND ENGRAVINGS

Atheneum · *New York*

1976

Library of Congress Cataloging in Publication Data

Hanser, Richard.
The glorious hour of Lt. Monroe.

SUMMARY: Traces the events of the Battle of Trenton
with emphasis on James Monroe's participation.
1. Trenton, Battle of, 1776
2. Monroe, James, Pres. U.S., 1758–1831
[1. Trenton, Battle of, 1776. 2. Monroe, James,
Pres. U.S., 1758–1831. 3. United States—History—
Revolution, 1775–1783] I. Title.
E241.T7H36   973.3′32′0924   75–13573
ISBN 0–689–30495–1

THIS BOOK IS FOR RICKY

CONTENTS

"It may be doubted whether so small a number of men ever employed so short a space of time with greater and more lasting effects upon the history of the world."

—George Otto Trevelyan
British Historian

I

THE LAST OF
THE COCKED HATS

ONE OF HIS COMRADES IN ARMS, a young artillery officer named Alexander Hamilton, had called him "a man of honor, a sensible man, and a soldier."

That was long ago, but James Monroe still looked the part. He was the fifth president of the United States now, and he was known as the "Last of the Cocked Hats"—the last of the men who had fought in the Revolution, and shaped the Constitution, and risen high in the government of the world's youngest nation.

He was in his sixties and in his second term of office. Official functions and affairs of state were routine with James Monroe, and he was used to receiving ambassadors and entertaining people of high importance in government and public affairs. But one evening, toward the end of his second term, he invited a man of no special importance in either government or business to have dinner with him in the White House. The presidential guest that night was named Lewis S. Coryell, and he came from a place called New Hope, in Pennsylvania, where he was active in the lumber business and in local politics.

3

Lewis Coryell never forgot that White House dinner. He remembered James Monroe as a tall, rather angular man who wore a white stock around his throat. He held his head high, and carried himself with all the dignity due his office. But he also had a surprisingly agreeable way about him. He put his visitor at ease.

Coryell noticed, too, that there was a certain awkwardness about the president, almost a shyness. This was strange because few men had ever won as many honors as James Monroe, or had less reason to be shy.

He had served in the Continental Congress, and was chosen governor of Virginia four times. He had been a United States senator, and then minister to France, Spain, and Great Britain. He was the only man who ever held two cabinet posts at the same time—Secretary of State and Secretary of War. He had been reelected to the presidency in 1820 without opposition, the only candidate to whom that ever happened except George Washington.

In view of all this, it took something of an effort for Lewis Coryell to recall that there once was a James Monroe quite different from the gray-haired and dignified statesman who sat across from him at the dinner table in the White House. Once there had been a young and adventurous James Monroe who had marched through the snow and sleet behind George Washington and who, with rifle blazing, charged against the Hessian cannon at Trenton in the battle that turned the tide of war and saved the Revolution.

That was nearly fifty years before, but that was what the president wanted to talk about with his visitor from Pennsylvania.

"As you know, Mr. Coryell," the president was saying, "I received a musket ball in my shoulder in the fighting in Trenton." He paused, and his right hand went up to the spot where the Hessian lead had entered his body. "I would have bled to death if a doctor had not been nearby and promptly taken up the artery. That man's name, I believe, was Riker— Dr. Riker.

"Now," said the President, "if I may ask it, I should like you to go about that neighborhood and make a proper search and inquiry for that doctor's descendants. If any such person should be found, I would like to know of it. If he should be deserving of it, and fitted for it, I should like to offer him an office in the government as a token of my gratitude."

Lewis Coryell was flattered to be given such an assignment, and he assured the president he would do his very best to carry it out. After he left, the president went to a White House window and looked out into the dark toward the Potomac. But his mind was on another river.

The Delaware . . .

II

THE SWORD
IS DRAWN

LEAVING HOME for the first time and going off to college is a major event in the life of any young man, but for James Monroe there was a special tingle of excitement to it. When he enrolled at the College of William and Mary in the town of Williamsburg, in the colony of Virginia, there was rebellion in the air.

In the streets and taverns there was an atmosphere of tension, as if something explosive might happen at any moment. This was the sultry summer of 1774, and enough had already happened to show that the winds of change were rising.

Storm signals were up. A hurricane was coming.

James Monroe was well aware of this as he registered for the first semester of the new term at William and Mary. He was only sixteen, but becoming a student at "The College" was a long step into manhood and maturity. It was also a mark of prestige and privilege. The school was almost a hundred years old, and it was the pet and pride of proud Virginia.

Monroe had never seen a bigger building than the broad two-story college structure with its high cupola and dormer windows, and its courtyard with trim gravel walks. It stood at one end of a mile-long street named for the Duke of Gloucester, the grandest thoroughfare in Williamsburg. At the other end loomed another imposing structure: the Capitol. On his first sightseeing stroll through the town, James Monroe stopped and stared at it for a long time.

There was a wall around it and on the front were the King's Arms, carved in stone and gilded, to remind everyone of the authority and might of Great Britain. Here, in this handsome edifice, was the source of the unrest that was seething in the town and throughout the colony.

Usually the place was alive with people coming and going, and elegant coaches clattered through the gates carrying distinguished citizens on important business. This was where the House of Burgesses met, the place where representatives of the people made the laws that governed Virginia. But now the Capitol was dark and lifeless. Its gates were closed, its doors bolted.

James Monroe knew why.

Not long before, the royal governor, Lord Dunmore, had dissolved the House of Burgesses. This was an outright insult to the people of the colony. But neither the people nor the burgesses were taking the governor's high-handed behavior meekly.

A few hundred yards along Duke of Gloucester Street, in the very heart of town, stood the Raleigh Tavern, which was the finest inn of the whole area. Fancy balls and grand dinners were usually held there, but now its white clapboards sheltered something else. It had become an unofficial capitol, a center for discussion and planning, where those determined to oppose the governor could meet and plan.

Upstairs, in a spacious chamber called the Apollo Room, the banished burgesses met in defiance of Lord Dunmore and his decree. Over their glasses of Madeira wine and tankards of ale, the burgesses puffed on their long clay pipes and talked and debated. Out from the Raleigh Tavern in Williamsburg went a call to the twelve other American colonies. "Let us," the call said, "come together and discuss our grievances."

The burgesses of Virginia were not calling for rebellion against the British crown. They were only asking for united action to protest against what one of their number—the tall, unsmiling burgess who represented Fairfax County—called "the violated rights of America." Others expressed themselves more eloquently or passionately, but George Washington's blunt phrase was sufficient. American rights were being violated. That was the issue.

Though a boy from the backwoods, James Monroe was more familiar with protest against injustice than many his age. His own father, Spence Monroe, had set an example for him. Almost ten years before, Great Britain had attempted to impose the Stamp Act on the colonies. The Act required everyone to attach revenue stamps to all legal and business papers—bills, deeds, wills, almanacs, pamphlets, newspapers, and even card and dice games.

This was a nuisance. Almost no business could be transacted without first buying and licking and sticking on a government stamp, though the tax itself did not amount to much and was not a heavy burden. What made the Americans boil was the fact that the Stamp Act was the first attempt by the British Parliament, acting for the king, to impose a direct tax on the colonies. The Americans had not been consulted. They were being taxed without their consent, and they objected furiously.

When a British army colonel named Mercer appeared in Williamsburg and announced that he had been appointed Distributor of the Stamps, a hostile crowd—a mob, really—formed around him and blocked his way on the street. He might have been physically attacked if the royal governor himself had not taken the Distributor of the Stamps into protective custody.

The next day Colonel Mercer resigned his office and withdrew. But even so the Capitol rang with a rousing speech of protest that thrilled the entire colony. It was delivered by a fiery young patriot named Patrick Henry, who had been a storekeeper and farmer but was now a lawyer and leader of the back-country people. In his attack on the Stamp Act in the House of Burgesses, Patrick Henry demanded that Virginia be allowed to make its own laws without interference from a king and parliament three thousand miles away in London. This brought cries of "Treason! Treason!" from some who heard the speech, but Patrick Henry had scored his point and would not be silenced.

James Monroe had been only a child then, but he could remember how his father had hurried off with other local patriots to a meeting place on the Rappahanock River where they all signed a petition against the Stamp Act. Spence Monroe was a friend and follower of Patrick Henry, and he had joined hundreds of other Virginians in a pledge not to buy any goods imported from England until the Act was repealed.

These protests and demonstrations took effect, and the Stamp Act was repealed, but the friction between the colonies and the mother country had not ended. Instead, a series of inflammatory incidents had kept the spirit of rebellion alive and burning.

When James Monroe was twelve, news had come down from the north about what happened in Boston one night in March of 1770. There had been a fist fight between a British soldier and a Boston workman one afternoon, and by nightfall bands of both citizens and soldiers were roaming the streets looking for trouble. At about nine o'clock, on King Street near the State House, there was a fracas involving a group of waterfront toughs and a British sentry. A threatening crowd had gathered. Soldiers of the guard were called out, but the crowd defied all attempts to disperse it.

A musket flashed and roared in the darkness. Others followed, and suddenly three Americans lay dead on the street. Two more were so badly wounded that they died not long after.

Exactly how or why the shooting came about was never entirely clear. Were the Americans who started the trouble true patriots boldly offering defiance to British authority? Or were they just a street mob on a boozy rampage? No matter; British troops had fired on American citizens and killed five of them. The affair became known as the "Boston Massacre," and another wave of outrage had swept through the colonies.

James Monroe had been in grammar school when news of the massacre came down the Atlantic coast to Virginia. He had been living then in a part of Virginia known as the Northern Neck. There was only one school in the whole region, but it was a good one. It was run by the local clergyman, a Scot whose name was Archibald Campbell.

To get to Parson Campbell's schoolroom every morning, James Monroe had had to tramp several miles through the woods with his books under his arm and his gun over his shoulder. As he made his way through thickets of pine and cedar, he never knew when there'd be a chance of a clear shot at a squirrel, a rabbit, or a partridge that might help fill the pot at dinner that night. Like the other boys at Reverend Campbell's school, young James could shoot, and climb, and swim, and find his way through the forest. Born far from the city, he was at home and at ease in the woodland.

James was tall for his age. He was sinewy and active, a good shot, a strong swimmer, and handy with horses. He lived on a little stream known as Monroe's Creek, which emptied into the Potomac. There was plenty of opportunity for a boy to roam, and explore, and hunt, and swim, and sail in the Northern Neck.

The Monroe family lived in a two-story frame

house that was bigger and more comfortable than those of some of his friends who lived deeper in the woods. James's father was a carpenter, or "joiner." That was a highly respected craft, and Spence Monroe was rated as a gentleman, the more so since the family owned about five hundred acres of land.

A special road called "Parson's Lane" had been cut through the woods to give access to the school, and James walked that road every weekday for more than four years. He did not always go happily. Archibald Campbell ran his backwoods academy as rigorously as if it were one of the world's great institutions of learning. Latin and mathematics were his specialities, and he drilled them into his pupils mercilessly.

The last year James spent at Archibald Campbell's school had been brightened by the arrival of a new pupil, who was soon his close friend. John Marshall (later to be the third Chief Justice of the Supreme Court) came from Prince William County, which was about fifty miles up the Potomac and real frontier country. There were no grammar schools there, so John's father sent him down to Reverend Campbell.

John had raven-black hair and intense, dark eyes, and was almost six feet tall. But the most striking thing about him was his high spirits. He was full of pranks and stories, and he and James made a curious pair. James was usually serious and not much given to easy laughter, while John was buoyant and merry more often than not.

Young Marshall held the other boys at Parson

Campbell's spellbound with his stories of hunting bear
with his father deep in the virgin forest and of how
huge slabs of the meat would be served up at family
feasts. Where John Marshall lived, they used thorns
for pins, there were no tablecloths, and when bear
meat or other game was lacking, everybody got along
on cornmeal mush and thought it no hardship.

John's father was a friend of George Washington and had worked with him as a surveyor. Like
James Monroe's father, the elder Marshall was a patriot and had been active in the opposition against the
Stamp Act and other oppressive measures of the British. He was a captain in the militia and he had taught
his son the basics of military drill and how to handle
both musket and rifle.

Young James was already keen for the patriot
cause, but he caught new fire from John Marshall. Together they talked endlessly about such thrilling out-
bursts of patriot zeal as the burning of His Majesty's
ship *Gaspée* up north in Narragansett Bay. She was
a revenue cutter whose mission was to run down
smugglers, but smuggling had become practically a
patriotic duty for Americans who resented paying
customs fees to the British. When the *Gaspée* ran
aground, the Rhode Island patriots boarded her, took
the crew captive, and burned her to the water's edge.

James Monroe was fifteen years old when word
of another event spread through the colonies. A galloping horseman, a silversmith named Paul Revere, had
brought the news from Boston to New York. From
there it was passed swiftly on to Philadelphia, and

then down to the Potomac and beyond. On December 16, in the year 1773, the Sons of Liberty had swarmed over three British merchant ships in Boston harbor and hurled 342 chests of tea into the water. The details were dramatic, and they supplied fodder for hours of excited talk among the boys at Parson Campbell's—and everywhere else. The Boston patriots had smeared their faces with soot and red paint, and put feathers in their hair, and carried tomahawks, and whooped like the Indians they were pretending to be. And they had a war chant to go with their costumes:

> Rally Mohawks! Bring out your axes
> And tell King George we'll pay no taxes
> On his foreign tea!

The whole event had gone off like a huge masquerade party. The British seamen had put up no resistance, there was no fighting, no one got hurt. After turning Boston harbor into an enormous teapot, the Mohawks had formed up in double ranks on the dock, shouldered their tomahawks and axes, and marched off in high style to a merry tune from a fife.

It looked like great good fun to many—another hearty twist to the tail of the British lion. That'll show 'em! But there was a deadly serious purpose beneath the horseplay and Indian whoops.

What prompted the Boston patriots to throw the British tea into the harbor was the same principle that had caused the uprising against the Stamp Act: a tax. The tax on tea was small, only three pence in a pound, but it was deliberately imposed to show the Americans that they were still subject to the decrees of Parliament, whether they liked it or not. True patriots saw this as "a diabolical project of enslaving America."

SPENCE MONROE died early in 1774. James's uncle, Joseph Jones, a judge and a member of the House of Burgesses, took the place of a father for young Monroe and became a model for him. The judge had a steady and upright character, and was a sturdy patriot. He arranged for young Monroe to enroll at the College of William and Mary in the summer of 1774. James was rawboned and gangling, with country manners and a boyish shyness that he never quite overcame. He was above medium height and had a rather large mouth that was agreeably set off by a straight, handsome nose. His speech, when he spoke at all, was slow and sparse, but his eyes were always clear and steady.

When James Monroe became a boarding student at The College, he intended to pursue the classical education for which Parson Campbell had been preparing him. He passed the entrance examination without difficulty, and set about acquiring the polish of a Virginia gentleman.

There were fewer than a hundred boys in the school. It was named for King William and Queen Mary who had granted its charter as the second college in the colonies, after Harvard. There were two stories, or legends, about its founding.

When an appeal for the charter was first made to

the king's attorney general, it was argued that the school would produce ministers who would save souls in Virginia. "Souls!" bellowed the attorney general. "Damn your souls! Make tobacco!" Tobacco was, indeed, the principal product of Virginia, the source of its wealth. When the school came into being, it was supported largely by tobacco taxes.

The other story was that, at the start, certain pirates who were on trial for their lives in London were persuaded to give part of their plunder to The College in exchange for lighter sentences.

All that had happened long before James Monroe's time and was ancient history to him and his fellow students. Of far more interest was the immediate situation at the school, where things were a good deal more lively than at Reverend Campbell's academy. Here the students kept race horses and fighting cocks. Some of the professors had even been brought up on charges of playing cards all night and "being seen drunken in the streets."

There was plenty of opportunity for a serious student to learn at The College, which had laboratory equipment for courses in science and astronomy that were in advance of their time. But the student body included many who thought of college mainly as a place for sport and entertainment. There was a rule against keeping guns and dogs in the living quarters, but not much attention was paid to it. Outside The College, the town of Williamsburg itself afforded all sorts of chances for fun and frolic—barbeques, dances, horse races, and gaming tables.

Life on the frontier had left James Monroe serious, anxious to be a part of a man's world. And it was a time for being serious. Monroe quickly formed an alliance with a fellow student named John Francis Mercer, who was the son of a wealthy planter from Stafford County. Mercer, too, was a budding patriot. Together the boys followed with the keenest interest every new development in the spreading rebellion against the rule of the British.

And the rebellion was growing on their own doorsteps...

SIX MONTHS after the Tea Party, its impact was felt directly in Williamsburg. Striking back at the unruly colonists, the British closed down Boston harbor. No ship could enter or leave the port. Even the ferry boats were forbidden to operate. The city was all but paralyzed.

Up to then the separate colonies had tended to concentrate on their own affairs and had largely ignored what was happening, politically and economically, in the others. But now a surge of support developed for Boston. Virginia sent cartloads of its Indian corn. Maryland contributed rye, pork, and bread. New Hampshire gave cows and money. A feeling of solidarity that hadn't existed before was growing in the colonies.

Not satisfied with punishing Boston, the British also issued a series of decrees intended to cow all Americans into obedience to the Crown. The political liberties of the people were curbed. Control over the courts by the British was increased. In the future, British soldiers would be quartered not only in taverns and empty buildings but in private homes as well.

Here were blows that struck at the freedom of the colonists in ways more obvious and immediate than even the taxation issue. The "Intolerable Acts," as the new measures were called, brought many more Americans into the ranks of the patriots. The strength of the rebellion grew accordingly.

The burgesses of Virginia voted that a "day of Fasting, Humiliation and Prayer" be observed throughout the colony in protest against the Boston Port Bill. It was this action that prompted Lord Dunmore to dissolve the House of Burgesses. And in September of 1774 the call went out from the Raleigh Tavern. From all the colonies except one, Georgia, delegates were soon on their way to Philadelphia for the first Continental Congress.

Williamsburg stirred with new excitement when the Virginia delegates to the Congress left to go north. There was George Washington, who was a familiar figure on the streets of Williamsburg but virtually unknown elsewhere in the colonies. There was Patrick Henry, whose eloquence would make him known as "a son of thunder." There were aristocrats like Richard Henry Lee and Peyton Randolph. And there were solid, practical men like Judge Joseph Jones.

His uncle's participation in the Congress at Philadelphia made the event particularly vivid for James Monroe. But the whole school was agog with what was happening outside the classroom. Most of the boys, and some of the professors, were eager patriots, but sentiment was by no means unanimous. Lord Dunmore's three sons were students at William and Mary, and there were a number of other boys who were hotblooded supporters of the Crown. In the general public there was a rift between the "radicals," who were keen for protest and patriotism, and the "namby-pambies," or conservatives. The same division between patriots and Tories was reflected in the student body.

But, of course, life at The College was not all politics and patriotism. When classes were over, the boys were free to roam at will through the town and its surroundings and take their fun where they found it. Visitors called Williamsburg "the finest town in Virginia," and some thought it the most attractive spot in America.

Scattered among the rows of white wooden houses were taverns, shops, and inns offering virtually everything a young gentleman might desire. There were sweetmeats from Barbados, and brandy from France, and corn liquor in abundance for coarser tastes. The menu of Virginia dishes was long, including a local speciality called Brunswick stew.

It was food, or the lack of it, that embroiled James Monroe and some of his schoolmates in a row with the college authorities. While it lasted, the ruckus inside the school made everybody forget the rebellion brewing outside. The issue was no such high-minded principle as taxation without representation. Instead, the boys charged they were being cheated on the meals being served in the Great Hall, where students and professors ate together.

The protest was touched off by James Innis, a student much admired for his swaggering boldness and dashing style. He got up a petition, which was signed by James Monroe and six others. It charged that the Mistress of the College, Maria Digges, was keeping "a sumptuous table of her own at the very time that Provisions in the Hall were scarce and intolerable." The accusation was that Maria Digges deprived the boys of delicacies they were entitled to and kept them for herself or her brother. She was also said to be selling meat and vegetables from The College to people of the town. For good measure, Maria was accused of "treating the Gentlemen of the College with scurrilous language."

Mistress Digges was called before a court consisting of the president of The College and all the professors and she denied everything. Among those examined was James Monroe, and his testimony was something of a surprise. He said he had never read the document in question and therefore couldn't prove a single statement in it. Why he signed it in the first place he never explained. He probably went along with the protest out of admiration for Innis, the campus hero.

The court found Maria Digges innocent of all charges, and scolded the students for bringing up the matter with so little evidence. The court also expressed alarm at the "ill humors and disorders that have crept into the college."

All was not as scholarly and gentlemanly at William and Mary as the president and professors could have wished. Students had stayed out at "unseasonable hours until some of them were drunk, which occasion'd a midnight disturbance in the College." Boys had been fighting and sometimes beating each other bloody with sticks and clubs. A college building had been badly damaged by vandals. And the president found it necessary to issue a stern warning against bringing arms and ammunition into The College.

But by the spring of 1775 there were good reasons for patriotic college boys to be storing arms and hoarding ammunition. Sensational news had come "by express"—by fast relays of galloping horsemen—from Boston, and from the towns of Lexington and Concord in Massachusetts.

War had begun.

On the village green in Lexington seventy-seven Minutemen had faced seven hundred British regulars and eight of the Minutemen had been shot down in their tracks. At a bridge over the Concord River, the local farmers had exchanged shots with the redcoats who had come to search their town for hidden arms. There had then been a running battle all that day between the withdrawing British and the American militia all the way back to Boston. But the heart of the news for every patriot in every colony was:

"We have fired on the king's troops!"

It was nine days before the story reached the South, and then the *Virginia Gazette* burst into print with a broadside that ended:

> The sword is now drawn, and God knows
> when it will be sheathed.

The news made a special impact on Williamsburg, which was going through a turmoil of its own. At almost the same time as the fight in the North, patriots had been on the march in Virginia, and among them were James Monroe and his schoolmates. In the rush of events outside The College, the squabble over food was forgotten and nobody any longer thought of heeding the warning against keeping firearms in the dormitories.

Now the College boys were carrying guns openly and proudly, to the beat of drums and the trill of fifes.

What set them marching in Williamsburg was another indignity inflicted on the people by the royal governor, Lord Dunmore. By night, under cover of darkness, a detachment of British marines landed from an armed schooner in the James River. They marched to an eight-sided brick building in the Market Square, near the center of town. This was the Powder Horn, or magazine, where the arms and ammunition of the colony were stored for use against possible Indian raids, slave uprisings, or local riots.

The marines began carting the kegs of gunpowder from the magazine to their ship. It was done because Lord Dunmore feared the people and what use they might make of the military supplies in the Powder Horn. But the secret operation was observed, and soon "drums were sent thro' the City" to alert the citizens to what was happening behind their backs. By dawn the whole colony was in an uproar.

Lord Dunmore had picked an explosive moment for his nocturnal raid on the people's arsenal. Not long before, in a church in Richmond, Patrick Henry had made another rousing speech to a convention of patriots and his words still burned in the ears of Virginians: "Give me liberty or give me death!" The people were in no mood to accept further assaults on their freedom.

It was Henry himself who led hundreds of armed citizens in a march to recapture the powder. A mass demonstration was staged on the Palace green, with boys from The College adding their voices to the general uproar. Lord Dunmore, shaken by the fury of the protest, backed down. He offered to pay for the powder if only order were restored. To save face, he outlawed Patrick Henry just as the patriot was about to set off for the Second Continental Congress.

After that, at William and Mary the classrooms were often empty. The lectures in rhetoric and moral philosophy were suspended or ignored. James Monroe and his roommate John Francis Mercer were caught up along with the others in the mounting turbulence of events. Without benefit of diploma, James Monroe was graduating into a world where scholastic background would count for less than courage, character, and faith in a cause.

Students were drilling on the College grounds now, and James got hold of a rifle and joined them. The leader of the campus patriots was, again, James Innis whose "warm and passionate temper" often got him into trouble with the school authorities but was no drawback for a drillmaster.

Military units were being formed all over the town. Besides the "College Company," there was a "Youth's Corps" of even younger patriots, and a band of "Williamsburg Volunteers." They were all spoiling for action, and in June of '75 James Monroe got a foretaste of what action might be like.

He was seventeen years old now, broad-shouldered, erect, and eager. And there was more fire and dash in him than his gawky exterior might indicate. When a chance came to take part in a foray against the Palace of the royal governor, he took it.

Lord Dunmore, near panic at developments in his domain, had withdrawn from Williamsburg and taken refuge aboard a warship on the York River. Behind him he left a palace full of arms guarded by a staff of loyal servants. A group of twenty-four patriots was organized to seize the weapons. James Monroe was the youngest of them. They made a surprise raid on the Palace, overpowered the servants, and scooped up all the arms in sight.

Monroe and his fellow raiders came away with 230 muskets, 301 swords, and 18 pistols. These they stored in the Powder Horn under guard, where the governor's men could not get at them and where they would be available to the patriots whenever needed.

After that armed patrols of patriots paced the streets of Williamsburg each night, and the place took on the look of an armed camp on the alert for an attack. A Committee of Safety took over the government. The break with Great Britain seemed complete. Virginia was not only in a state of insurrection, but well on the road to full independence.

Then, one day in the fall of 1775, the town, which had thought itself ready for anything, was shaken by a sudden invasion. A band of whooping frontiersmen, who at first were mistaken for Indians, came swarming through the streets. They wore fringed trousers made of deerskin and long linen hunting shirts dyed brown. Buck tails decorated their hats, and their hair fell to their shoulders. On every shirt the words "Liberty or Death" were spelled out in white thread. In their leather belts were long hunting knives and tomahawks. They were nicknamed "shirt-men," but they were the Culpeper Minutemen who had marched one hundred miles to Williamsburg from the back country.

At the head of their column the shirt-men carried the rattlesnake flag with its legend: DON'T TREAD ON ME. For them, and others like them, the rattlesnake was the proper symbol of the frontier. It was peculiar to America; it did not strike until provoked; it gave warning before it hit; and when it hit it was deadly.

The Culpeper Regiment had come to Williamsburg at the summons of Patrick Henry, who wanted it on hand to counteract whatever move Lord Dunmore might be planning against the patriots. But when they arrived, the shirt-men learned that the governor had fled and was gathering his forces at Norfolk, the largest city in Virginia and its chief port. With barely a break in stride, the shirt-men set off for Norfolk with the long, ground-eating gait of the frontier.

But before they went, James Monroe had a warm reunion with one of them. John Marshall was a lieutenant of the Culpeper Minutemen. Not only was John an officer of the troop, but so was his father, Thomas. Together, father and son, they marched off to do battle at Norfolk.

James Monroe watched them go with a pang of envy. Though sleepy Williamsburg had of late come alive as a center of patriotic resistance, it was not where the fighting was.

III

" 'TIS TIME

TO PART"

—Tom Paine

It was the first people's army in history, if you could call it an army at all.

After Concord, where the Minutemen and militia shot the British almost to pieces on their retreat to Boston, there was a surge of patriotic pride and activity throughout the colonies.

On May 10, 1775, the Second Continental Congress had opened in Philadelphia. Five days later it passed a resolution putting the colonies officially in a state of defense.

Minutemen and militia began streaming toward Boston from all over Massachusetts, and also from New Hampshire, Rhode Island, and Connecticut. They were farmers, and fishermen, and shopkeepers, and laborers, and young men who didn't yet know what they were except Americans. They came in their shirt-sleeves, and in homespun woven by their womenfolk, and in every kind of working clothes, and sometimes in ragtags of old uniforms.

Those that had weapons brought them, for there was no army arsenal to supply them. They carried old firelocks and fowling pieces over their shoulders

and powder horns on their hips. Some of them still
had the manure of the barnyard on their boots. Israel
Putnam, who was gray-haired but hard as hickory,
had been plowing his field in Connecticut when he
heard the news of Lexington and Concord. He left
plow and oxen standing in the furrow and set straight
off for Boston. Before long he would be one of the
boldest generals in the people's army.

Other men came trudging into camp with six or
eight or ten followers straggling behind them and
called themselves captains of their own troops. For
many it was the first time they had ever come into
contact with a man from another colony.

The British were astonished when this helter-
skelter swarm of citizens in arms formed a ring
around Boston, penning the redcoated army inside.
"What?" exclaimed Major General John ("Gentleman Johnny") Burgoyne in disbelief. "Ten thousand
peasants keep five thousand of the king's troops shut
up?" He couldn't believe it and he wasn't going to
stand for it. But the "peasants" turned out to be harder
to cuff aside than Gentleman Johnny and his kind
could imagine.

The British found this out in June when patriots
dug themselves in atop a hill that overlooked the city.
(The place was called Breed's Hill, but for some reason the battle that ensued was named after nearby
Bunker Hill.) The best troops in the British army
were dreadfully mauled in trying to drive the Americans off. Three all-out assaults were made on Breed's
Hill, and when they were over nearly one thousand

of the king's troops lay dead or bleeding on the American earth. Though the British captured the hill in the end, the Americans won the glory. The British commander was called home in disgrace.

Next month the encampment outside Boston was set buzzing by the arrival of an imposing group of horsemen. The soldiers were expecting their new general, but nobody had ever seen a picture of him and nobody knew what he looked like. As the horsemen rode by, however, the men picked out their leader at once. Nobody had to tell them which one it was that the Continental Congress had sent to them as "General and Commander in Chief of the Army of the United Colonies."

It was, of course, George Washington. He sat his horse like a commander and he had the unmistakable bearing of a leader. Even in England, when the word reached there, the newspapers spoke of his "martial dignity." One of them wrote that any king in Europe would look like a valet next to George Washington.

As a Virginian, a plantation owner, and the foremost soldier of the South, Washington filled the requirements for commander in chief of the army better than anyone else available. Besides, as a Connecticut delegate pointed out, he was "no harum-scarum ranting Swearing fellow, but Sober, steady and Calm." The vote for him was unanimous.

Another vote of the Congress touched the life and career of James Monroe. A resolution was passed that read:

"That six companies of expert riflemen be immediately raised in Pennsylvania, two in Maryland, and two in Virginia."

Unlike the militiamen who joined up for short periods and went home almost whenever they liked, these new soldiers enlisted for a year's service. They became the nucleus of the Continental army. They were the beginnings of all the United States armies to come.

James Monroe was one of them.

NOBODY WAS GOING to class at William and Mary any more. One by one, in the fall of 1775, the students dropped out, discarding their books to shoulder arms. Three of their professors joined them. The College was "essentially shut up by the procession of the war," as Monroe afterwards described the situation. In January of 1776 he volunteered for army service, and he did it, he said, "with enthusiastic zeal."

His friend and roommate, John Francis Mercer, "and several other youths of great merit" went with him. They all joined the Third Virginia Regiment as cadets. A cadet was a young gentleman who served in the ranks with the expectation of getting a commission, and Monroe's was not long in coming.

He was only eighteen years old, but he was the stuff of which officers were made. He was strong, steady, and intelligent. His background qualified him as a gentleman, and he had connections. His uncle, Judge Jones, was a man of influence, and he no doubt did what he could to advance the career of his favorite nephew. And at this stage of the army's growth there was a shortage of good officers. Not long after he joined the regiment, James Monroe was made a lieutenant in the company commanded by Captain John Thornton.

It was a rifle company, and this made it a special and significant unit not only in the new American army but in the history of war as well. In the age of the musket, soldiers with rifles were strange and startling newcomers to warfare. No other army in the world had them. They were uniquely American, products of the new land's limitless forests and wild frontiers.

The rifle was not invented in America but was improved and perfected by American craftsmen. As brought over from Germany years before the rebellion, it was heavy, short-barreled and clumsy. Gunsmiths in Pennsylvania and later in Kentucky skillfully reshaped and streamlined this unlovely weapon. They made it slimmer and longer, lighter to carry and easier to handle. They adapted it for use in hunting in the American woods, increasing its range and accuracy. In the end, they produced the graceful and efficient weapon that became known as the "Pennsylvania," and also "Kentucky," rifle.

What made the rifle different from the traditional musket was that spiral grooves were tooled along the inside surface of the barrel. These grooves imparted a spinning motion to the bullet when fired, and this greatly increased the range and accuracy of the weapon. The smooth-bore musket could shoot less than half the distance of a rifle, and was nowhere near as accurate.

Hundreds of boys growing up in the American backwoods learned to handle the gun almost as soon as they could walk. The daily pot-shooting of racoons and turkeys and squirrels developed skill of eye and hand; and by the time the boys were twelve or thirteen many of them were expert hunters. A new breed of woodsmen and Indian fighters emerged, and among them were the best marksmen in the world. It was natural then to make these dead-eye frontiersmen into soldiers when war came, and accordingly the special rifle companies were organized.

The American rifleman had a powerful psychological effect on the enemy, as George Washington shrewdly sensed. He issued an order encouraging the "use of Hunting Shirts, with long Breeches made of the same cloth . . . it is a dress justly supposed to carry no small terror to the enemy, who think every such person a complete Marksman."

Washington regarded the riflemen as a form of what we now call "psychological warfare." He had reason for his belief. In the retreat from Concord to Boston, many a redcoat was hit or killed by an enemy he could not see and at whom he could not shoot back. Militia and Minutemen fired from behind trees and walls and rocks, often with an accuracy that was new and terrifying to the British. "What an unfair way to fight a war!" one English officer complained.

Sentries who were accustomed to walk their posts in confidence, sure that no musket ball could reach them, were now being dropped in their tracks from impossible distances by "shirt-tailed men with damned twisted guns." Officers were especially vulnerable, since the sharpshooters took malicious delight in picking them off, which was also considered by the British to be a most dastardly thing to do.

In the battle of Breed's Hill, the British were appalled to see an American marksman standing on something in a trench and calmly shooting down at them. He hit twenty officers without missing a shot. The marksman did not take time to reload. After every shot he handed down his empty rifle to someone in the trench who handed up a loaded one. It took a whole company of grenadiers firing at him steadily with their old-fashioned muskets to put that one man out of action.

Before the battle was over, every officer on the staff of the attacking general was either dead or wounded, without exception. The white breeches of the general himself were splattered red with blood.

It was no wonder that an Englishman who had seen these marksmen in action wrote to the military authorities: "In marching through the woods, one thousand of these riflemen would cut to pieces ten thousand of your best troops." Unfortunately for the Americans, the war was not to be fought in the woods or from behind trees and rocks. But at the start, riflemen made an unsettling impression on both enemy and friend.

Most of them were over six feet tall. All of them were tough as old leather and quick as cougars. They all carried tomahawks and the long "scalping" knife

which was the woodsman's all-purpose implement.
Famous as Indian fighters, they themselves often
behaved more wildly than any Indian. They were a
law unto themselves, and they soon became a disrup-
tive element in the camp. They took orders from no
one and refused to perform the routine work of the
soldier. If one of their number was sent to the guard-
house, the others broke in and released him. They put
everybody on edge with the random popping of their
rifles and they picked fights right and left.

Washington himself had to break up a brawl
between the frontiersmen and a band of Marblehead
sailors from Massachusetts. The commander in chief,
towering over all of them, waded into the melee and
began cracking heads together until order was restored.

From being hailed as incomparable assets to the
rebel cause, the frontier riflemen were soon being
shunned as nuisances. One report said that Washington openly expressed the wish they'd never come. And
they were the least of his problems.

Washington's headquarters were in the home of
the president of Harvard, but there was nothing aca-
demic about the problems he faced. The situation, he
said, was "little more than a mere chaos." Nothing was
organized, nothing was working right, everything
was in short supply. He had been assured that 308
barrels of powder were available to him in case fighting should break out. In fact, only 36 barrels were
available, less than nine rounds to a man! He was so

dumbfounded at learning this that "for half an hour he did not utter a word."

There was little discipline among the troops, hardly any at all by Washington's rigid standards. Americans, by and large, scorned military rules and procedures. They often elected their own officers, and then ignored them. Washington was dismayed at the laxity that prevailed even in the officers' corps. Once he came across a cavalry officer "unconcernedly shaving one of his own men"!

Still, many good and patriotic men were shouldering their own muskets, determined to march behind Washington wherever he might lead. Some of them were shouldering not muskets but rifles and, unlike the wild frontiersmen, were learning to use them as disciplined soldiers in orderly units.

Among them was Lieutenant James Monroe of the Third Virginia Regiment.

LEAVING SCHOOL to join the army was not at first as great a leap for him and the other young gentlemen from William and Mary as they had expected. When a long roll on the snare drum woke them up in the morning, they found themselves, as soldiers, just about where they had been as students.

The encampment where recruits were being trained was on the grounds right behind The College. The spot had been chosen by Colonel Patrick Henry when he was put in command of all Virginia troops. For James Monroe, John Mercer, James Innis, and the other new-made soldiers, the day was no longer parceled out in lectures, relaxation, and study. It was divided up by drumbeats. The drum told them when to get up, paced their steps at drill and called them to retreat at sunset when the day's duty was over. It beat tattoo for "lights out" and sleep.

Here there was less haphazard milling about, less laxity and confusion, than at Cambridge. A measure of military order prevailed in the Virginia regiments, and it increased with time.

In James Monroe's unit, the Third Virginia Regiment of Foot, the standard dress was the fringed hunting shirt, which had to be uniformly cut and colored. The appearance of officers and men was regulated in every detail: hair was to be cut short, everybody's at exactly the same length, and combed; beards closely shaved; shoes cleaned; and hats "cocked on one side," according to orders.

Such details might seem trivial to the troops, said an Order of the Day, but they "tend to give what is call'd Esprit de Corps without which Regiments never grow to Reputation." Officers and men alike were expected to prepare themselves in every way to "defend the darling Rights of Liberty and the property of their Country."

Early in the year of '76 the talk of the camp, and the colony, was all of "Little Bunker Hill," the battle at Norfolk that brought the shooting war to the South. For James Monroe, the story came directly from his friend John Marshall who had been in the midst of it.

The Culpeper Minutemen had marched to Great

Bridge, twenty miles from Norfolk. There Lord Dunmore had thrown up fortifications and manned them with British regulars and volunteers loyal to the king. This was in an area called the Dismal Swamp, and it could be reached only by causeways on either side.

The situation was especially tense and ugly because Dunmore tried to start a slave uprising by promising freedom to any black man who would fight on his side. Racial fears and hatreds were added to emotions already murderously explosive. Some blacks joined the Royalist cause but most did not, though the promise of liberty must have been tempting to many.

Unable to attack without cannon, the Culpeper patriots threw up breastworks of their own, sat back, and waited. They outwaited Lord Dunmore, whose nerve broke first. He ordered an attack—probably, as John Marshall thought, "because of that contempt for Americans which had been so freely expressed in the House of Commons."

British grenadiers, six abreast, advanced along the causeway with fixed bayonets. And, said Marshall, "the bravest of the Americans rushed to the works where, unmindful of order, they kept up a tremendous fire on the front of the British column." The commander of the grenadiers, a Captain Fordyce, won everybody's admiration, even his enemy's. As Marshall told the story afterwards, the British officer "marched up under this terrible fire with great intrepidity until he fell dead within a few feet of our breastworks."

Then the British column broke and fled back to

its own fortifications, leaving the field to the Americans who had not lost a man.

The Minutemen marched on to Norfolk where Dunmore and his staff withdrew to warships in the harbor. Unable to reach the British in any other way, the Americans amused themselves by taking potshots at the men-of-war from the shore.

This stung Lord Dunmore into another one of his foolish and headlong actions, and he ordered his ships to bombard the town. The cannonading, by more than a hundred guns from three warships, lasted for nine hours without a break. Then the British regulars landed and set fire to what remained of the town. They burned it to the ground.

A British midshipman who saw it all made an entry in his diary for January 9: "The detested town of Norfolk is no more!"

Nothing the British had done so far was as ruthless, and as senseless, as the wanton destruction of one of the foremost towns of America. And it had the opposite effect from what Lord Dunmore intended. Far from intimidating the South, it added momentum to the rebellion. "We are only sharing part of the sufferings of our American brethren," wrote one citizen of Virginia. "We can now glory in having received one of the keenest strokes of the enemy without flinching."

Still aglow from the glory of the Great Bridge and Norfolk, John Marshall was greeted like a hero by the cadets of the Third Virginia when he joined

them, along with his father, Thomas. By becoming
officers of the regiment, the Marshalls made the transi-
tion from militia, which consisted of local, part-time
soldiers, to Continentals. By order of Congress, the
Virginia regiments had been made part of the Continental Line. They were what we would now call
federal troops, or regulars.

Young Marshall would have been an asset to any
outfit lucky enough to get him. Besides his qualities
as a soldier, proven now in actual combat, he was also
a morale factor of considerable value. He made jokes,
he laughed a lot, but he was also a splendid physical
specimen. He could run faster and jump higher than
any of the others; they called him "Silver Heels" because of it. He could usually outpitch his friend James
Monroe in their quoit games, and outshine him at other
sports, but the two remained good friends.

In March of '76 more thrilling news came down
from the North.

The British evacuated Boston.

Hemmed in by George Washington's improvised
army, the English were threatened with destruction
when rebel cannon were mounted on heights overlooking the city. The guns were some that Ethan
Allen and his Green Mountain Boys had captured at
Ticonderoga, and now they threatened to pound the
English to pieces. Caught in an impossible position,
the redcoats boarded their transports and sailed away.

The great port city of Boston was purged of the
British without a battle. George Washington had his

first triumph as commander in chief. He then wheeled his army around and marched south to New York City.

Something even more powerful than guns and gunpowder was working to destroy the colonial system in America while Washington marched south. This was a pamphlet of forty-seven pages called *Common Sense*, written by a man named Tom Paine. Few books ever published have made such an impression on the public.

In hard, hammering language that everyone could understand, *Common Sense* laid out the arguments for separating the American colonies from their mother country. With arguments that allowed no compromise, Tom Paine attacked the idea of a huge country like America submitting forever to the rule of a small, faraway nation like England. "There is something absurd," said *Common Sense*, "in supposing a continent to be perpetually governed by an island. In no instance has nature made the satellite larger than its primary planet." He dismissed King George III, whom many Americans were still regarding as their lawful ruler, as "the Royal Brute."

To answer the argument that, after all, the colonies had so far prospered under English rule, Paine wrote: "We might as well assert that because a child has thrived upon milk that it is never to have meat . . ." It was the immensity of this country, and its possibilities, that Paine stressed over and over. On the final page of *Common Sense* was printed a single line in strong black letters:

THE FREE AND INDEPENDENT
STATES OF AMERICA

The pamphlet was snatched up by the thousands.

And what *Common Sense* so eloquently urged was actually happening. More and more, the term *colony* was being discarded in favor of *state*. Both North and South Carolina cut their ties to Great Britain. And for the men of the Virginia regiments, James Monroe included, there was news closer to home that gave new spring to their step at drill and a new lift to the chin on parade.

The news was that the Virginia Convention had voted unanimously "to declare the United Colonies free and independent States." This resolution, coming from the largest and most populous colony, made a thunderous impression. The bell in the tower of the Burton parish church in Williamsburg pealed out the news, and the British flag atop the State House was torn down. A new American banner with thirteen stripes was hoisted in its place.

That was on May 15, 1776, and the next day the troops paraded smartly through the streets in celebration. The resolution was read out to the people, and afterwards some wealthy citizens "made a handsome collection for the purpose of treating the soldiery." As toasts were drunk to "General Washington and victory to the American arms," cannon boomed and the men jubilantly fired off their muskets and rifles.

Next month at the Continental Congress, it was Richard Henry Lee of Virginia who introduced an-

other historic resolution. It said that the colonies were now "absolved from all allegiance to the British Crown, and that all connection between them & the State of Great Britain is, and ought to be, totally dissolved."

What remained to be done was to draw up the final and definitive document that would declare the independence of all the colonies to all the world. This, as the document itself would say, was required by "a decent respect to the opinions of mankind."

Thomas Jefferson of Virginia wrote it in two weeks, from "When, in the course of human events . . ." to ". . . we mutually pledge to each other our lives, our fortunes, and our sacred honor." In between, in wonderfully clear and forceful language, he listed twenty-seven abuses against freedom and humanity which the king and Parliament had inflicted on Americans and which they proposed to endure no longer.

The Declaration of Independence was debated and discussed at length amid the heat and flies of midsummer Philadelphia, and in the early days of July, in the year of 1776, it was formally accepted by the Congress.

There was many a parade and many a bonfire throughout the colonies—the *former* colonies—when news of the Declaration spread. In New York City, a roaring mob of soldiers and citizens smashed the statue of George III on the Bowling Green and melted it down for bullets. The Assembly of South Carolina spoke for many by greeting independence "with unspeakable pleasure."

In Williamsburg, James Monroe turned out with his regiment to parade and fire off salvos when the Declaration was read to the people at the Capitol, the Court House, and the Palace. The Virginians, though, had already had their own Independence Day in May, and to them many of Jefferson's famous phrases in the Declaration had a familiar ring.

The famous phrases, in fact, often had less to do with creating enthusiasm for the cause than history books afterwards indicated. Many years later, a veteran of the Revolution named Levi Preston was interviewed on what made him fight. He gave some surprising answers.

"Why did you go?" he was asked. "Histories say you men of the Revolution took up arms against intolerable oppressions."

"Oppressions?" said Levi. "I didn't feel them."

"What, weren't you oppressed by the Stamp Act?"

"I never saw any of those stamps. Never paid a penny for one of them."

"Well, what about the tea-tax?"

"Tea-tax! I never drank a drop of the stuff."

"Then I suppose you had been reading philosophers like Locke and Harrington on the eternal principles of liberty?"

"Never heard of 'em. We read only the Bible, Watts's *Psalms*, and the Almanac."

"Well, then, what was the matter? And what did you mean in going to fight?"

"Young man," replied Levi Preston, "what we

meant in going for those redcoats was this: we always had governed ourselves, and we always meant to. They didn't mean we should."

Old Levi's idea of what was worth fighting for did not, after all, differ very much from Thomas Jefferson's . . . or James Monroe's. All such men—Levi, Thomas, James, and the hundreds like them—could differ on shadings and detail but still agree with Tom Paine that "The Sun never shined on a cause of greater worth." That belief sustained the patriots of the Revolution through hardships, doubts, and dangers that tested faith and endurance to the utmost.

MARCHING ORDERS for the Virginia regiments were expected momentarily.

The Articles of War were read out before every company every morning. At drill and on parade the drums were beating more insistently, the fifes were shriller. The men were giving more care and attention to their weapons and equipment.

For James Monroe and the other riflemen in his regiment, it was a time of tense preparation. The musket was the army's standard weapon, and the rifle was still regarded with scepticism. For the traditionalists who make up the majority in every army, the rifle still had to prove itself.

Most of the men, like Monroe, had brought their own weapons with them and were used to handling them on the hunt and at target practice. But it took time and training to accustom young men to the idea

of using them not to pop at chipmunks and wild tur-
keys but to kill another human being. Granting the range and accuracy of the weapon, sceptics stressed its disadvantages in combat. For one thing, it took almost three times longer to load a rifle than a musket.

American riflemen often molded their own lead balls and made them slightly smaller than the bore of the weapon. They carried a supply of these balls in leather pouches, along with their powder horns. They would pour a charge of powder down the barrel of the rifle while it stood upright on its stock on the ground. They would then place the ball on a greased patch of cloth, put this on the opening of the barrel, and jam it down with an iron ramrod.

Sometimes the ball and patch did not slide down the barrel far enough and had to be hammered home with a wooden mallet, which riflemen carried for this purpose. In order to take full advantage of the rifling in the barrel, and to get maximum range and accuracy, the ball had to fit tightly and snugly in place. Otherwise some of the force that expelled it from the barrel would be lost, reducing its speed and range. This factor was not so essential in a musket, which, consequently, could be loaded more quickly and fired with greater rapidity.

With powder and ball in place, the gun was discharged through the operation of an ingenious device called the flintlock. Its function was to cause a flint to strike against steel, thus creating a spark that exploded the powder in the gun. This mechanism was practically the same for both rifle and musket.

The flint was held in a tiny vise on the end of what was called the cock. Getting ready to fire, the soldier pulled the cock back against a spring until it caught and was latched into place. When the trigger was pulled, the latch was released and the spring sent the cock plunging against a piece of steel called the frizzen, or hammer.

The frizzen flew back and the sparks from the blow showered down on a receptacle called the pan, which held a small quantity of priming powder. A flash resulted, and this spurted through a touchhole on the side of the barrel which exploded the main charge inside. And that explosion sent the ball hurtling from the barrel with a sharp report like the crack of a bullwhip.

Once the trigger was pulled, whether on rifle or musket, the flintlock reacted with much greater speed than it takes to describe it. There was a momentary gap between the time the trigger was pulled and the explosion inside the barrel, but it was only a brief hesitation. For all practical purposes the actions were simultaneous.

Sometimes, of course, the flint failed to spark when hitting the frizzen. Or the priming powder in the pan might be damp and fail to ignite. Or the touchhole might be stopped up. Misfire. No bullet issued from the gun. But the flintlock mechanism worked far more often than not, and the ball that came whistling from the barrel of a Revolutionary rifle, or musket, could kill or maim the man it hit just as surely as the bullet from a modern machine gun.

Lieutenant Monroe and his fellow riflemen regarded themselves as an elite corps because their weapon could do things that were beyond the scope of any musket. But contrary to lore and legend, the Revolution was fought, like the other wars of the time, mainly with the musket and not the rifle.

Muskets were more sturdy and less easily put out of action by the weather. A seasoned soldier could load and fire off his musket four or five times a minute while the best riflemen could manage only one or two shots in that time. In the smoke of battle it was difficult to take proper aim with the rifle, which canceled out one of its main advantages. Muskets were not aimed but only pointed in the direction of the enemy at close range. Their effect came from disciplined troops firing in steady volleys.

Another crippling drawback to the rifle was that it had no bayonet, which made it virtually useless in many situations as battles were then fought. The standard maneuver, as executed by the British, was for the infantry to advance to within fifty yards of the enemy, or less, and deliver one or more volleys. Then the troops charged with their bayonets and settled the issue in hand-to-hand combat. The bayonet, called "the white weapon," was the most effective and terrifying item in the British arsenal. Its cold steel extended twenty-one inches beyond the top of the musket, which itself was almost five feet long. The combination made a most formidable assault weapon.

It could both stab and slash and cause dreadful wounds and multiple deaths in the hands of well-trained and ruthless troops, which the British were.

The Americans, at the start, were unused to the bayonet and only learned to use it, and counter it, gradually. Without the white weapon, riflemen could not deliver a charge or withstand one. They were seldom placed in the line of battle for that reason, and also because their loading and firing were so slow. Instead, they were used as special troops—skirmishers, flankers, sharpshooters, and pickets.

This was the kind of action that Lieutenant Monroe and his comrades were looking forward to. There were two contradictory traits in Virginians that almost every outsider noted. One visitor saw them as "indolent, easy, and good-natured"; but in the next breath he was speaking of them as "jealous of their liberties, impatient of restraint." They were, said another observer, touchy and quick to anger, with "an eagerness for physical encounter which seems to pervade the whole population."

When the summons to war came to the Virginia troops, the orders read: "The Third & 6th Regiments to hold themselves in readiness to march at a moment's notice."

Lieutenant Monroe's unit was the first to go. Early one August morning a cannon boomed in the camp and the "General" call was sounded on the drums. The six-man tents were struck, folded, and loaded on wagons, one to each company. Blankets were in short supply and some of the soldiers had only rugs for night covering, but they went on the wagons too, along with tools, rations, and reserve ammunition.

The wagons moved off the parade ground to their assembly point where the baggage train was being formed.

The men hastily stuffed their haversacks with odds and ends of personal belongings, extra clothing, rations, and eating utensils. The haversacks were large canvas envelopes painted red on the outside and carried on the left hip from a strap slung over the right shoulder. They were the soldier's personal supply kit.

When the drums beat "Assembly," the various companies lined up according to the seniority of their captains. Lieutenant Monroe took his station in the Fourth Company commanded by John Thornton, a passionate patriot from Culpeper County. Once, in a church in Fredericksburg, Captain Thornton had dragged a minister down from his pulpit and kicked him out of the church because of a sermon that preached submission to taxation and the king.

Twice again the cannon sounded, and drums beat "March," and the ten companies of the Third Virginia Regiment of Foot stepped off smartly on their way to battle. If there was urgency, and even haste, in the movement of this column of some seven hundred officers and men, there was good reason for it. A British fleet had appeared off Sandy Hook, in New York, and was landing troops in overwhelming numbers.

George Washington's army was threatened. The Revolution was in danger.

The march route went through the town of Fredericksburg. Beyond the town the regiment passed through territory familiar to Lieutenant Monroe: the Northern Neck. Keeping pace with his company permitted him no time for contact with family, friends, or places cherished from his boyhood. The situation allowed for no lag in the progress of the column.

The Third Virginia crossed the Potomac and slanted east and north through Maryland. The ordinary marching pace of the army was 120 steps to the minute, and each company had one drummer and one fifer to set the rhythm of the march. But the route cut through country that was mostly wooded and unsettled. The roads were hardly more than wagon tracks and often they were nonexistent.

Parade-ground formations could rarely be maintained, and there were long breaks in the drumming and fifing while the drummers and fifers rested, or were too occupied, like the others, in forcing their way along tangled forest paths. The drums were used chiefly to keep segments of the column in contact with each other. If advanced elements got too far ahead, drummers in the rear sounded "three long runs" until the column closed up again.

Lieutenant Monroe and his fellow riflemen served as scouts who went in advance of the column to feel out the terrain and bring back information. They also made sure there was no ambush ahead into which the column could march unaware. They were the eyes of the regiment. The riflemen were also used as flankers, marching parallel with the main body of the column and about a hundred yards from it on either side.

What the army called "hard bread," usually known as hardtack, was the basic food for the marching men, along with salt pork. But these were soldiers who, mostly, were at home in the woods and able to live off the land as they went. For them it was no feat to bag fresh game along the way and to skin it and cook it over the evening campfire. When opportunity for relaxation occurred during the rare breaks in the march, a favorite sport was throwing tomahawks against trees, competing with each other for accuracy and distance.

The march that began in the heat of August found a tinge of autumn crispness in the air as it worked its way north. The fringed hunting shirts of the troops were often soaked with the chill rains of early fall. Private Joseph Blackwell, of Captain Chilton's Tenth Company, came down with severe chills and fever and had to be left behind with friendly farmers until he could recover and rejoin the regiment. But few men dropped out, despite the steady strain of rapid, daylong marches over nearly five hundred miles of difficult terrain.

On the way a new commander was appointed for the Third Virginia. He was Colonel George Weedon, who was called "Old Joe Gourd" by the troops because he was supposed to use such a ladle when serving punch in his tavern in Fredericksburg.

The British found it amusing, and contemptible, that rebel officers were often anything but professional soldiers. Henry Knox, chief of artillery for the Continental army, was a Boston bookseller; Brigadier John Glover was a fisherman; Major General John Sullivan was a lawyer. And so it went, to the snickers of the enemy.

But Old Joe Gourd had been a captain in the Virginia militia and fought in the French and Indian War, and so had credentials as an officer. He was, besides, a friend of George Washington, of Thomas Jefferson, and of Patrick Henry, all of whom patronized his tavern. Washington used to play cards there and once wrote in his diary: "lost, as usual."

As the Virginia troops crossed into Pennsylvania and swung east toward New Jersey, all the news that reached them was bad. On August 27 the first major battle between the British and the Continental army under George Washington was fought on Long Island. It was a disaster. Afterwards an English officer wrote: "Rejoice! We have given the Rebels a d——d crush!"

He was right. Outnumbered, outmaneuvered, and outfought, the raw and untrained Americans had been cut to pieces by the disciplined British formations. Three hundred were killed and more than one thousand taken prisoner, a fearful toll. Only a skillful withdrawal by Washington under cover of fog and rain saved his army—and the cause itself—from total annihilation.

Lieutenant Monroe and his fellow Virginians got

only confused fragments of the story as they pressed on to New York. The reports of the Continental losses were disturbing enough, but an unfamiliar word gave an especially ominous ring to the scraps of information that came to the column on its way. The word was *Hessians!*

As the column approached New York, the reports on the situation in the city grew more and more ugly. The place was riddled with Tories and treason; the mayor had been arrested and jailed. And there was the incredible story of a plot on the life of George Washington himself. A member of his own bodyguard, Sergeant Thomas Hickey, had been hanged in public for his part in a conspiracy aimed, it was said, at kidnapping or assassinating the commander in chief.

And now the city was being threatened with capture by the greatest expeditionary force ever sent across an ocean. Washington wanted to burn the place down to keep it from becoming a permanent base for the British. Congress would not allow him to put this "scorched earth" policy into effect, but that the idea was proposed at all indicated how desperate the situation was.

When the Third Virginia Regiment of Foot reached the city on September 12, officers and men were "in good spirits and generally healthy," as one of them said, despite the long grind of the march. "Great joy was expressed on our arrival," wrote Captain John Chilton in a letter home. He was not exaggerating.

These, after all, were George Washington's own

people. He had known many of the officers before the war. He had fought side by side with some of them in the Virginia militia against the French and Indians. He had spent social evenings with them in the Raleigh Tavern in Williamsburg and at Weedon's in Fredericksburg. They were people he could depend on as men and as soldiers. At this point he badly needed that kind of assistance.

Only recently he had written to Congress: "With the deepest regret I am obliged to confess my want of confidence in the generality of the troops." The cherished idea that a citizen-soldier fighting for his freedom would prove a match for any mere professional had been shattered on Long Island. There whole units had run. Many had surrendered needlessly. But here were rugged Virginians who, in contrast to most of his other troops, were well trained, disciplined, and eager for action. It was a relief to welcome them to his line of battle.

The Third Virginia was deployed on high ground in upper Manhattan. The plateau stretched across the island between the Harlem and Hudson Rivers and was called Harlem Heights. Washington was straining to bring his sick and wounded, along with his supplies and cannon, into this new position when the British struck again.

A man named Jacobus Kip had a farm on a cove in the East River, in Manhattan, about where East 34th Street now ends. It seemed a likely landing place, one of many, for the British across the river on Long

Island. About five hundred raw militia troops from
Connecticut were strung along the shore there in shallow trenches. One of the defenders was Joseph Plumb
Martin whose memoirs would one day be published
under the title of *Private Yankee Doodle*. On Sunday
morning, September 15, he suddenly heard "such a
peal of thunder from British shipping that I thought
my head would go with the sound."

He made "a frog's leap" into a ditch, and when
he dared to peek warily over the rim he saw five British frigates in the river, all of them letting go at him
full blast with all their cannon. That was not the worst
of what Private Martin and other Connecticut militiamen saw. The river was clogged with flatboats and
sixteen-oared barges, all of them headed straight for
the cove of Jacobus Kip.

The defenders cowering in their trenches were
mostly farm boys who had never fired a shot at anybody and had never had anyone shoot at them. What
they saw shook them to their shoes. Some of the barges
were packed with strange-looking men in blue uniforms who were singing loudly in an unknown
tongue. They were Hessians, and they were singing
hymns in German to nerve themselves for the assault.
The sound, somehow, was even more unsettling than
the continuing thunder of the cannon. The other boats
and barges were crammed with red-coated grenadiers
who looked like giants in their towering headgear. In
the shallow water near the shore, they climbed out of
the boats, methodically formed into line, and advanced

on the shallow trenches in a solid wall of scarlet. Their bayonets gleamed and flashed in the bright morning sun.

Between the head-splitting bombardment, and the blue-coated foreigners bellowing hymns, and a wall of oncoming bayonets, the Connecticut farm boys did not hesitate. They scrambled out of their useless trenches and ran. "They did not tarry to let the grass grow much under their feet," was the way Private Yankee Doodle remembered it. As he took to his heels like everyone else, he noticed that "the ground was literally covered with arms, knapsacks, staves, coats, and hats."

Not a shot was fired at the enemy. There was only panic and flight.

When Washington heard what was happening, he galloped to the scene at once. He could not believe what he saw. Wild-eyed men, including their officers, went streaming past him panting with fright. They paid no attention to his shouted orders that they take cover behind walls and fences, and fight back. In his fury and dismay, he lashed out at them with his riding whip. That did no good either, and in complete frustration he took off his hat and slammed it on the ground.

"Good God!" he roared. "Are these the men with whom I am to defend America?"

At a crossroads, in the general confusion, Washington suddenly found himself alone. About eighty yards away was a platoon of British soldiers coming on the run. Motionless astride his horse, the commander remained frozen to the spot, as if defying the advancing enemy to do their worst. They came closer and closer, and still Washington did not move.

At the last moment, his aides came galloping up and seized his bridle. Then they wheeled his horse around and led him quickly out of harm's way. To Nathanael Greene, one of his generals, the episode had a chilling implication. George Washington, thought Greene, was "so vexed at the infamous conduct of his troops that he sought death rather than life."

IV

HEIGHTS
AND DEPTHS

JAMES MONROE'S REGIMENT was spread out in a line among the rocks and trees and boulders of Harlem Heights. It had no part in the calamity down below at Kip's Bay. But Monroe and his comrades heard about it quickly enough. They were outraged.

"Disgraceful" and "dastardly" was what they called the behavior of the militia who had run away. The Virginians assured each other that when their chance came, they would behave far differently from "those cowardly Yankeymen." Their chance was not long in coming.

The high ground on which they were posted was in plain sight of the enemy lines. "We can see belches of fire from their encampments at every discharge," reported Captain Chilton of the Tenth Company who kept writing home despite all the clatter and confusion of the camp. For the benefit of the civilians back home, he added "the thundering cannon" to the background noises of his letters. (Not everyone was so conscientious about writing home. Captain Chilton had to apologize for one of his men. "Johnny Blackwell was just about to write when he was ordered on guard.")

Since they arrived, the Virginians had been paraded, and marched and countermarched, sometimes at three o'clock in the morning. Then they were sent back to their camps. No particular purpose seemed to be served by these exertions but, as the few veterans among them knew, this was the way armies functioned, even in the face of the enemy.

"We every hour expect to be in action," Captain Chilton wrote, "but we're not sure whether we will be attacking them, or they us." Though everybody was expecting action, the Virginians found themselves in the midst of the Battle of Harlem Heights almost before they knew what was happening.

Something was going on down below, beyond a mile-wide depression called the Hollow Way. The British had troops there, hidden from view by dense woods. General Washington had to know whether the enemy was massing for an attack and, if so, where and when it might come. Skilled and reliable scouts were needed to find out what was happening beyond the Hollow Way. Fortunately, Washington had them.

They were called Rangers and there were about 140 of them, mostly from New England regiments. Every man was hand-picked for his courage, initiative, and his willingness "to serve either by water or land, by night or by day." Their leader was Thomas Knowlton, from Ashford, in eastern Connecticut. His men adored him.

They boasted that he was an officer who never

said, *"Go* on, boys!*"* but always *"Come* on, boys!*"*
And he looked like a hero. He was six feet tall and
slim, full of energy and sinewy strength. Cool but
fierce in battle, he was amiable and polite to everyone
when the shooting was over.

He was a lieutenant colonel when he took his
Rangers out on reconnaissance before dawn on September 16. He led them across the Hollow Way and
up through the woods on the other side. Feeling their
way toward the main body of the British, they came
upon pickets of an enemy outpost and shots were
exchanged.

Alarmed, the British sent out several hundred of
their light infantry in support of the outpost while
the Rangers kept up a brisk fire from behind a stone
wall that served for breastworks. More redcoats came
up and joined in the skirmish. Outnumbered many
times over, and with some of his men dead and
wounded, Colonel Knowlton broke off the fighting
and withdrew in good order, mission accomplished.

At headquarters on the Heights, Washington and
his staff heard the firing but could not be sure what
it meant. The army was alerted, the troops got under
arms. Presently, through his glass, Washington could
see advance elements of the enemy light infantry
come into view on the opposite Heights. The general
was undecided what to do. He seemed reluctant to
order an attack, the situation being uncertain.

Just then, loud and clear from the British side, a
bugle call pierced the morning air. It was not a call to
the troops to advance, or halt, or deploy, or retreat.

In fact, it was not military at all. Instead, it was a fox-hunting call, the one that announces that the fox has been run to earth, ready for the kill. Washington, a fox-hunting man himself, instantly recognized it for the insult—the taunt, the jeer—that it was intended to be.

So did his aides.

"I never felt such a sensation before," said Colonel Joseph Reed, the general's adjutant. "It seemed to crown our disgrace."

The Rangers had, in fact, pulled back in good order, but their withdrawal was being ridiculed as another American flight from battle. Coming on top of the real humiliation at Kip's Bay the day before, the bugle call was too much to bear. Something would have to be done to make the British pay for their insult.

Rather than retort with an attack, which his weakened army could not sustain, Washington resorted to deception. He set a trap.

He sent a detachment of infantry into the Hollow Way with orders to keep up a brisk musket fire as they went. This provoked a response from the British, as it was intended to do. They sent their light infantry forward to meet the supposed attack, and additional troops came up in support. This fell in with Washington's plan; the more of the enemy that entered the valley the better.

Then he moved to spring his trap.

He ordered three companies of Virginia riflemen to swing around the right flank of the British under cover of woods and rocks. Their mission was to get behind the British in the valley, cut off their retreat, and so force their surrender.

The flanking party included Captain Thornton's company of the Third Virginia, with Lieutenant Monroe as one of its riflemen. It was his first experience of battle, his first exposure to the possibility of sudden death from an enemy. It was his first occasion to discharge his rifle with intent to kill.

All his life he remembered the stealthy passage across the eastern edge of the valley and through the woods that led to a place called Vandewater Heights. With his comrades, he worked his way up to the other side of the valley where he knew the enemy to be.

The flanking party was under the overall command of Colonel Knowlton, and it included most of his Rangers. The Virginia troops were commanded by one of their own, Major Andrew Leitch. Like Knowlton, the major was a brave and spirited officer, one of the best in his regiment.

While the diversionary fire-fight continued in the Hollow Way, the flankers moved, tense and silent, along the enemy's right. They worked yard by yard toward a rocky rise from which they could sweep around behind the British, closing the trap. They were not far from their objective when something happened that ruined the whole enterprise. Through error, or perhaps the sudden loss of nerve on the part of an edgy junior officer, the order to shoot was given prematurely. The sharp, crisp crack of rifles betrayed the presence of the flankers and alerted the British to their danger. They fell back to a vacant field, took position behind a fence, and began firing from there. The flanking party pressed forward, keeping up an aggressive fire of its own. A hot engagement developed.

Then misfortune struck the Americans again.

Major Leitch mounted a rocky ledge to survey the situation and was hit three times in quick succession. One musket ball entered his groin and two pierced his belly. He was carried off the field, mortally wounded.

Within ten minutes, Colonel Knowlton, totally indifferent to danger as usual, climbed the same ledge for the same purpose—and was immediately hit in the small of the back. One of his captains caught him as he was falling, and asked him if he was badly hurt. Knowlton said he thought he was. The captain was astonished at the coolness of his colonel, who was obviously in great agony. The captain heard Knowlton dismiss his plight with the words: "I do not value my life if we do but get the day." In an hour he was dead.[1]

Now there were no senior officers to command the flanking party. Only captains were left to guide and rally the men. The loss of both Major Leitch and

1. Colonel Knowlton would have been comforted to know that one of his descendants, William A. Knowlton, would also become a distinguished officer in the American army. In 1973, as commandant of West Point, Lieutenant General Knowlton spoke at the 197th anniversary celebration of the Battle of Harlem Heights.

Colonel Knowlton could have been shattering to the morale of the troops, an excuse for the sort of panic that spread at Kip's Bay the day before. But on Harlem Heights the Yankee Rangers and the Virginia riflemen kept up their pressure on the enemy instead of running away from him.

Lieutenant Monroe was in the midst of that action and remembered the incident vividly. "On the fall of Maj. Leitch and Col. Knowlton," he recalled afterwards, "our corps retired about two hundred yards. We then rallied and returned to the action, which we sustained a considerable time, completely checking the progress of the enemy." The sight of Americans standing, fighting back, and even advancing astonished the British and added to their confusion.

"Great gallantry" was the phrase Monroe used to describe the behavior of his comrades that day on Harlem Heights. And gallantry was needed. The heaviest fighting came at noon, and by this time the British had thrown in some of their most formidable troops. To the wild skirling of their bagpipes, the Forty-Second Highlanders—known as "The Black Watch"—came running into the fight in their parade uniforms, not having had time to change into battle dress. The Virginians had never seen soldiers in skirts and bare knees before, and the fierce Scotsmen in their kilts and tartans and black bonnets were a further test of nerve and stamina for the raw American troops. The fighting was hottest in a buckwheat field, about where West 120th Street runs today. It was there that

the Virginians, for the first time, came face to face
with the enemy who would be their special antagonist
from then on: Hessians.

Though the British had purchased them like cattle at so much a head (about thirty-five dollars) these
German hirelings were among the best soldiers in the
world, and the most feared. They were trained, disciplined, and went into battle according to regulations
laid down by one of history's great war lords, Frederick the Great. They took their name from the
province of Hesse, in Germany, from which most of
them came.

Totally indifferent to what the war was about,
most of the Hessians thought of their service in
America as a chance to enrich themselves with plunder. They had been told by their officers that the
Americans were barbarians who gave no quarter, and
they themselves killed any prisoners they took. A
deep and lasting dread of the mercenaries seeped
through the American ranks.

In the buckwheat field on Harlem Heights, the
Hessians came in two colors—blue and green. The
blue were the crack infantrymen known as grenadiers,
the same hymn-singing assault troops that had terrified the defenders at Kip's Bay. The ones in green
were *Jägers*, pronounced "Yayger," which meant
huntsmen or chasers. At home they had all been for-
esters or hunters, and their military calls were blown
on hunting horns. They were among the most formidable soldiers of their time, and they were the only
ones on the British side who used both rifle and

bayonet. The Hessian rifle was a short, stubby model, not as accurate or effective as the tall Kentucky but a dangerous weapon nevertheless.

In the clash on Harlem Heights, not even the *Jägers* with their rifles and bayonets intimidated the Americans. In addition to the Virginia Regiment, which was now engaged both on the flank and in the center, fresh units from Maryland and Massachusetts were thrown into the fight. They pressed on "with splendid spirit and animation," as one observer noted, and in the end the Americans were treated to a sight none of them had ever seen before.

They saw British soldiers withdrawing . . . they saw the *backs* of redcoats!

But now General Washington had reason to fear that the British, to retrieve the situation, would bring up a large body of reinforcements. This would change the picture entirely and, perhaps, overwhelm the relatively skimpy American forces. The general's military secretary, a Philadelphia patriot named Tench Tilghman, was sent to call off the advancing Americans.

"The pursuit of a flying enemy," Tilghman reported, "was so new a scene that it was with difficulty our men could be brought to retire. But they gave a *Huzza!* and left the field in good order."

IT WAS NOT REALLY much of a battle, as historic battles go. "A pretty smart skirmish," Tench Tilghman called it, and that was about right if only its military importance was considered. But its morale value was tremendous.

"You can hardly conceive the change it has made in our army," Joseph Reed wrote to his wife. "The men have recovered their spirits and feel a confidence which before they had quite lost." Eighteen hundred Americans had faced the best the British could throw against them without flinching. In two hours of hard combat, sometimes at only forty yards, they had driven the enemy from the field—for the first time. Even the brigade that disgraced itself at Kip's Bay the day before had given a good account of itself.

For the Virginians it had not been a question of recovering confidence but of testing themselves. Harlem Heights was their baptism of fire and they had come through it proudly. Almost before the last wounded came limping from the battlefield, and while vultures were still circling over it, the good news was on its way back to Williamsburg. "Old Joe Gourd"—Colonel Weedon of the Third Regiment —sent off a report to the president of the Committee of Safety back home. The English, he wrote, had "got cursedly thrashed." He was entitled to brag a little since he himself was in the thick of the fight. The hilt of his sword had been shot away by a British musket ball.

James Monroe had reason to congratulate himself, too. He had behaved well in his first battle, and he had had his first taste of victory. The day after the battle there was the additional thrill of hearing his own unit given special mention when George Washington's general orders were read out to the troops. On that day the password in the American lines was

Leitch, in honor of the officer who had been triply
wounded in leading Monroe's detachment against the
British and was now dying.

If Harlem Heights proved that Americans could
match courage and skill with the British on the battlefield, it proved something more as well. The victory
had been shared by troops representing all sections of
the country. Washington himself, like other southern-
ers, was inclined to look down on the New Englanders. But Colonel Knowlton and his Rangers were
among the best troops in the whole army and had
distinguished themselves again at Harlem Heights. In
his general orders, Washington referred to Colonel
Knowlton as "one who would have done honor to any
country."

After that there was a good deal less sneering at
the "Yankeymen." The war was bringing the people
of the separate states together and making them aware
of their common nationality.

Neither side had gained any ground on Harlem
Heights, so the lines were the same as when the battle
started. "We are now very near neighbors, and view
each other every hour in the day," Colonel Weedon
reported. "A general action is every hour expected."

But nothing happened.

The sluggishness of the British command in the
American rebellion is one of the puzzles of history. A
bold, driving general might well have destroyed the
Revolution before its first year was out. Military ex-
perts agree that the whole Continental army could
have been captured, or wiped out, after its disaster on

Long Island if the British commander had pressed his advantage as energetically as other generals have done in similar situations.

Fortunately for America, though, the British general was Sir William Howe. He was called "the most indolent of mortals," a man who did everything too late. He was tall and swarthy, an impressive figure. He had distinguished himself fighting the French in Canada, but in America he operated only in fits and starts, losing one glittering opportunity after the other. Characteristically, he lapsed into one of his spells of inactivity after the repulse on Harlem Heights. He did not resume the offensive for a month.

The Americans, of course, did not know they had been granted a reprieve. They were kept in a constant state of alarm, on the expectation that an attack might come at any time. Lieutenant Monroe and his comrades were put on what they called "exceeding hard duty" as pickets, guards, and foragers. This, coming on top of the long march from home and the immediate battle, gave them all an unforgettable initiation into what army life could be like in the field.

ON HARLEM HEIGHTS, too, they had another experience they didn't soon forget. They watched New York burn down.

The men on guard saw the sky to the south begin to glow on the night of September 20, and at first they stood and wondered what in the world could be causing it. The glow spread and brightened until it seemed that the whole sky had somehow caught fire.

Only one thing could possibly cause such a blaze: the city itself was going up in flames.

"A most tremendous blaze," said a witness inside the city, as a brisk wind spread the flames from house to house until about five hundred caught and burned to the ground. How it started no one knew, but the British assumed it was a work of sabotage by the rebels. A suspect was knocked down by a patrol of soldiers and thrown into the fire to burn to death. Another man was accused of cutting the handles off water buckets to make them useless. He was hanged, first by the neck and then by the heels.

The British were furious because the blaze destroyed hundreds of houses they had intended to use for quartering their troops. Washington had wanted to burn the place down himself for this very reason—to make it useless to the British as winter quarters. He did not conceal his pleasure. "Providence, or some good honest fellow, has done more for us than we were disposed to do for ourselves," he said.

As weeks went by with no action developing, the troops on Harlem Heights occupied themselves by trying to make living conditions a little less rugged. Monroe and his comrades went searching for wood—planks, if possible, for the shacks they were knocking together against the increasing chill of autumn. Encamped between two rivers, they tried to vary their diet with catches of fish, but without much luck. Pork and beef were often available in that farming country, along with cabbages and apples. Foraging parties ventured far afield—sometimes "in the teeth of the Enemy," as John Chilton wrote—without drawing fire. The British seemed "vastly busy" at some project or other, but nobody knew what.

While waiting for something—anything—to happen, the men had plenty of time to talk about the war and speculate on its length and outcome. All of the men had by now experienced the power of the British Crown, personally and directly, in one way or another. Almost everyone had comrades, relatives, friends, or acquaintances whom the British Crown had done to death by bullet, bayonet, or cannonball. Everyone realized that mighty stores of British power were still in reserve.

Not since Rome had the world seen an empire that reached so far and hit as hard as Great Britain. She was mistress of all the oceans. She had come victorious out of the Seven Years' War with France. She had wrested Canada from the French. She dominated North America. She was mistress of fabled and far-off India.

Motivating the British was a powerful will to win and a habit of winning. "We live by victory," said the English general Sir Henry Clinton, who warned his countrymen to "avoid even the possibility of a check." To the British military it seemed an absurdity that the pitiful, ragtag American army should challenge the might of the British empire. The Americans, after all, had no military tradition, no discipline, no training, and, in the opinion of the British, were not even a nation.

Still, the advantages were by no means all on the

side of the mother country. Three thousand miles of ocean stretched between the English coast and the American shore. Every single soldier and all his arms and supplies had to be shipped across that wide wilderness of water—shoes, uniforms, musket balls, cannonballs, tents, belts, buttons, much of his food, some of his fuel, almost everything needed to keep him alive and fighting. Adverse weather delayed the ships for months. Storms blew them off course and sometimes sank them. There was no refrigeration and fresh food was impossible to carry. Troops sickened and died on the way, or were unfit to fight when they did arrive.

On sheer numbers, the odds were all against the Americans. Great Britain was a nation of eight million people with enormous resources, one of history's best armies, the most powerful navy in the world. In manpower, she outmatched America four to one.

There were only 2,500,000 Americans, and they were sprinkled along a coastline of more than a thousand miles. About 500,000 were slaves who had no pressing interest in supporting the American cause, though many did so. And great quantities of goods on which the Americans depended had to be imported —mostly from England.

Still, as even the minor engagement of Harlem Heights showed, Americans under good leadership were capable of beating British regulars. The Americans were motivated by intangible factors that tended to outbalance even the weightiest of England's material advantages.

The American was fighting on his own soil. In
contrast to the British grenadier, or the Scottish High-
lander, or the German mercenary, he knew the
ground he was fighting for and loved it. He was at
home, and that made an enormous difference. The
enemy fought largely because he was ordered to and
for no other reason. The American patriot had an
ideal—independence, freedom from foreign domina-
tion. That alone was a motivating force powerful
enough to keep the Revolution going in the face of repeated setbacks and disasters.

Most of Washington's men were farmers, or
workmen, or tradesmen, and not professional soldiers
at all. Except for clergymen, every able-bodied free-
man between the ages of sixteen and sixty had to drill
with a militia unit. He had to supply his own gun and
ammunition and enroll in the company of his town-
ship. The idea was to provide local protection against
possible Indian raids or slave uprisings.

Militia units were not designed to stand up to
regulars in formal battle, and they often showed
themselves incapable of doing so. Discipline was not
severe. Training was seldom sufficient. Militiamen
were citizen-soldiers, and they were usually a good
deal more of the first than the second.

But if the Americans were less disciplined than
their foe, they often showed more initiative and were
more self-reliant. From the start, there was something
that could be called "the American spirit," and it baf-
fled the European military mind. The Prussian drillmaster, Baron von Steuben, learned to admire it

when he came over to train American troops later in the war. He put it this way:

"The genius of this nation is not in the least to be compared with that of the Prussians, Austrians, or French. With them, you say to your soldier, 'Do this,' and he does it. But here I am obliged to say, 'This is the reason why you ought to do that'—and then he does it."

George Washington's dream was of an army that would be "a band of brothers, willing and ready to die for each other." Once, in a talk to a regiment he said: "Quit yourselves like men, like soldiers, for all that is worth living for is at stake!"

That was the spirit in which hundreds of eager young men like James Monroe and John Marshall volunteered to fight. But they soon discovered that the actual fighting was almost the least of the ordeals they had to face.

The army seemed to be in a constant state of chaos and disintegration. There was never enough of anything. Once the grand and inspiring declarations had been made, the Continental Congress seemed to lapse into almost total incompetence and confusion. Everything was always in short supply—clothing, powder, bullets, tents, shoes, even guns—everything an army needs to survive and function. There was no uniformity of dress or equipment. Some units were smartly turned out and well drilled, like Smallwood's Maryland Rifles, and the Delaware Continentals, and some of the Virginians. But most of the soldiers had no uniforms at all.

The pictures we now see of Continental soldiers in neat blue tunics and cocked hats are largely the creation of artists long after the war was over. Ordinary civilian clothes were what most of the men were wearing when they faced the British in their resplendent red coats or the Hessians in their blue and green. Knee breeches, long stockings, cowhide shoes, and round hats with broad brims were the American style. As the war went on and clothing was in even shorter supply, men were reduced to rags and had to wrap themselves in blankets—when they had blankets.

SIR WILLIAM HOWE had been rather surprised by the stand of the Americans on Harlem Heights, and when he made his next move it was a cautious one. He did not risk a frontal attack. Instead, he slipped an amphibious force up the East River under cover of fog and landed four thousand troops at a place called Throg's Neck. This was a peninsula in Long Island Sound to the rear and left of Washington's position. The maneuver threatened to cut off the Americans and squeeze them to death in a British nutcracker.

Washington and his army were saved from possible disaster by a handful of Pennsylvania riflemen—thirty in all. They had spotted the landing, and with deadly accurate fire from behind a woodpile they stopped the entire British advance in its tracks. It was a superb example of the devastating effect the American rifle could have in expert hands and of the frontier style of fighting. The Pennsylvania rifles delayed the British long enough, and disrupted their plans sufficiently, to give George Washington the time he desperately needed.

Aware that the British could not be held up indefinitely and that his position was now untenable, Washington decided to withdraw to the north. On October 18 he abandoned Harlem Heights and began a twenty-mile retreat to the village of White Plains.

It was a long and laborious haul for a disorganized and underequipped army of thirteen thousand men. There were not enough wagons and horses to move the supplies, cannon, and ammunition. The carts and wagons carried loads partway, dumped them, and went back for more. It took four days to cover ground that should have required only a single day.

For Lieutenant James Monroe it was a bewildering experience. His initiation into battle had been a small but exhilarating taste of victory. But now a puzzling stalemate was being broken by an equally puzzling retreat. Whatever had been gained by the skirmish on Harlem Heights had obviously been canceled out; a success had degenerated into a reverse.

But for Monroe and his company the retreat was partially redeemed by an unexpected action on the way. To protect his right flank, Howe had sent a detachment to hold the village of Mamaroneck, on the road to White Plains. The troops chosen for this mission were the notorious "Queen's Rangers," a unit composed of Americans loyal to the king. Their commander was the redoubtable Major Robert Rogers, a bold and passionate Tory. This had come to Washington's attention, and he decided something must be done to clear the way for the retreat of his troops.

The raid on the Queen's Rangers was commanded by Colonel John Haslet of the Delaware Battalion. It included some Maryland troops and also the company of Captain John Thornton of the Third Virginia, to which James Monroe of course belonged. All together some 750 patriots marched by night against the Tory camp.

They descended on the enemy bivouac at about one o'clock in the morning. They slipped past the first sentries but roused a second picket line, and a wild moonlight melee broke out. Colonel Haslet was wounded in the shoulder, and Monroe's company commander took charge. Once again the Virginians were in the forefront of the fight.

Above the bang of musket and crack of rifle the cry of "Surrender, you Tory dogs! Surrender!" could be heard. Some of them did. Before the patriot troops were beaten off, thirty-six Loyalists were taken prisoner, and twenty were killed. The booty included sixty muskets, sixty precious blankets, and two battle flags. American casualties amounted to three killed and twelve wounded.

Once again Lieutenant James Monroe was involved in a close-combat engagement and came away unscathed while some of his fellows were left dead on the field. He was becoming a seasoned veteran.

WHEN JOSEPH PLUMB MARTIN from Connecticut, otherwise known as "Private Yankee Doodle," got to White Plains he did what most of the soldiers did in

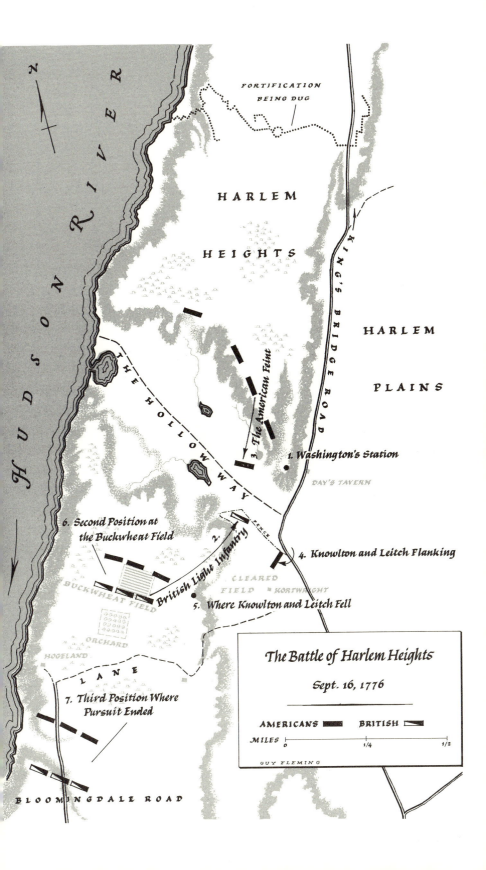

FORTIFICATION
BEING DUG

HARLEM

HEIGHTS

HARLEM

PLAINS

The American Feint

3.

1. *Washington's Station*

DAY'S TAVERN

6. *Second Position at*
   the Buckwheat Field

2.

4. *Knowlton and Leitch Flanking*

British Light Infantry

CLEARED
FIELD ⋅ KORTWRIGHT

BUCKWHEAT FIELD

5. *Where Knowlton and Leitch Fell*

ORCHARD

HOGELAND

L A N E

7. *Third Position Where*
   Pursuit Ended

HUDSON RIVER

THE HOLLOW WAY

KING'S BRIDGE ROAD

BLOOMINGDALE ROAD

The Battle of Harlem Heights

Sept. 16, 1776

AMERICANS ▬▬▬   BRITISH ▭▭

MILES ├———————————┼———————————┤
      0   1/4   1/2

GUY FLEMING

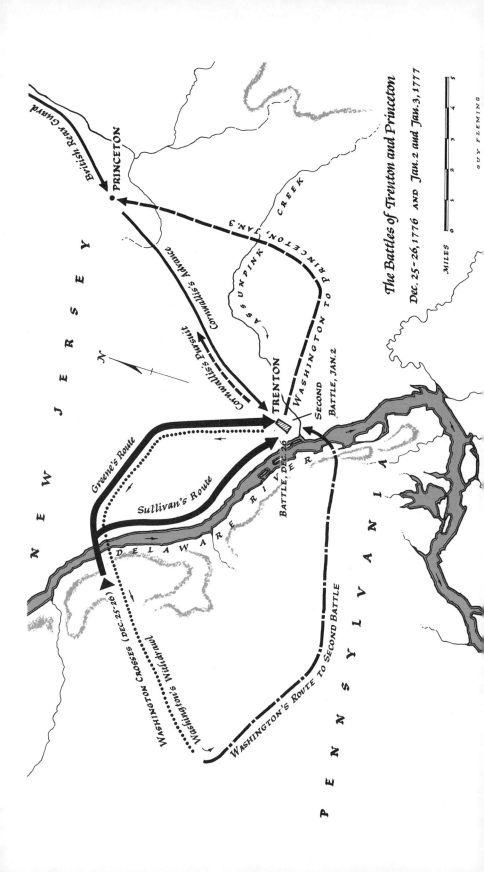

The Battles of Trenton and Princeton
Dec. 25-26, 1776 and Jan.2 and Jan. 3, 1777

GUY FLEMING

MILES

NEW JERSEY

PRINCETON

British Rear Guard

Cornwallis's Advance

Cornwallis's Pursuit

WASHINGTON TO PRINCETON, JAN. 3

ASSUNPINK CREEK

TRENTON

SECOND
Battle, JAN. 2

WASHINGTON TO PRINCETON, JAN. 2

Greene's Route

Sullivan's Route

BATTLE, DEC. 26

DELAWARE RIVER

N

WASHINGTON CROSSES (DEC. 25-26)

Washington's Withdrawal

WASHINGTON'S ROUTE TO SECOND BATTLE

PENNSYLVANIA

This is the earliest known portrait of James Monroe. It was painted some time after he served in the Revolutionary Army, perhaps while he was studying law with Thomas Jefferson. The artist is unknown. *Courtesy James Monroe Law Office and Memorial Library, Fredericksburg, Va.*

A view of the College of William and Mary, established in
1693, as it must have looked to James Monroe when he enrolled in 1774 at the age of sixteen. *Courtesy New York Public
Library Picture Collection.*

Kepp's Bay (1778) by Archibald Robertson. (Unfinished
sketch, drawn two years after the Kip's Bay Landing with
the five British warships penciled in.) Swarming across the
East River in flatboats, the British and their Hessian mercenaries landed in Manhattan, at Kip's Bay, on September 15,
1776. A terrific bombardment from the enemy frigates
shattered the morale of the raw Connecticut troops defending
the shore. They broke and ran without firing a shot. *Courtesy
Spencer Collection, New York Public Library.*

At the Battle of Harlem Heights, on September 16, 1776, the
42nd Highlanders—the famous "Black Watch"—were thrown
into action in their dress uniforms. Here the Highlanders are
withdrawing under the American assault. It was the first time
that Continentals drove British troops from the battlefield.
Courtesy New York Public Library Picture Collection.

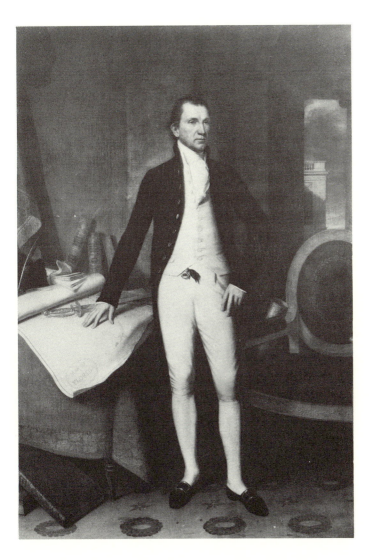

James Monroe as president. Painted by John Vanderlyn about
1820. *Courtesy New York City Art Commission.*

In the most famous picture ever exhibited in America —
Emmanuel Leutze's *Washington Crossing the Delaware* — Lt.
James Monroe is standing next to the General and carrying
the colors as the leading boat nears the Jersey shore. Lt.
Monroe did in fact make the crossing and fight heroically at
the Battle of Trenton, but he was not in the same boat with
Washington. He crossed several hours before the General did.
And he could not have carried that flag because it had not
yet been designed. The crossing was made at night, in storm
and dark, and not in broad daylight as the painting has it.
Both Washington and Monroe had grown up on rivers and
knew about boats; neither would have been so foolish as to
stand up during a stormy crossing. The river in the picture

is not even the Delaware, but the Rhine, since Leutze painted the scene in Düsseldorf. (A German, he had grown up in Philadelphia and returned to his native country where he completed the picture in 1851.) The figures in the boats are mostly Americans whom Leutze persuaded to pose for him as they passed through Düsseldorf. The figure of James Monroe is based on sketches previously made by the artist. Monroe's place of honor in the lead boat was a result of his heroism at the Battle of Trenton. If many of the details of the picture are wrong, the spirit and drama of it have pleased Americans for several generations. *Courtesy of the Metropolitan Museum of Art, Gift of John S. Kennedy, 1897.*

"A glorious day for our country!" said George Washington when the Hessians surrendered at Trenton. The artist's conception of the scene is dramatic but not very accurate. Col. Rall, badly wounded, was dying in agony and did not formally hand his sword over to George Washington, as pictured here. The demoralized Hessian units surrendered piecemeal. But the result was the same: A great victory was won. *Courtesy New York Public Library Picture Collection.*

their spare time. He looked for food. He and some friends found a field of English turnips and immediately began to pull them up. They cut off the tops, and gnawed greedily at what was left. After stuffing themselves, they carried away as many as they could while the owner of the field wasn't looking.

By this time, Private Yankee Doodle was enough of a veteran to know how to take care of himself when the commissary fell down on the job, which it constantly did. Congress had established a food ration for the troops and it included a pound of bread, a pound and a quarter of beef or pork, a pint of milk, and some other items. The joke was that all this was to be provided "if the goods may be had."

They seldom were.

The turnips at White Plains were tasty, but Private Doodle didn't get much of a chance to eat them. Back at camp, he found the troops lined up on parade and was told the British were coming. He threw his surplus turnips into his tent, grabbed his musket, and fell into the ranks.

"Before we were ready to march," he remembered, "the battle had begun."

At White Plains the British staged a battle spectacle such as the Americans had never seen before. The target of their attack was Chatterton's Hill, which dominated the field. The Americans held it; the British wanted it.

First their artillery bombarded it, and one of the defending militiamen was killed by a cannonball. This caused some panic and confusion, but there were resolute Continentals defending the hill as well, and they held steady.

On the plain below, it looked as if the entire British army was advancing. One American officer was awestruck by the sight. "It was truly magnificent," he said. "A bright autumn sun shed its luster on the polished arms; and the rich array of dress and military equipage gave an imposing grandeur to the scene as they advanced in all the pomp and circumstance of war."

The Americans defended their hill with courage, but in the end the weight of the attack was overwhelming. The British swarmed up on all sides, while their artillery kept pounding out a path for the advancing troops. At one point, a detachment of light dragoons—mounted soldiers—came bursting into view and joined the attack. Their trumpets sounded the charge, their kettle drums beat a booming tattoo, and their sabers flashed and glittered as they came thundering at the goggle-eyed Americans.

The charge of the galloping horsemen terrified the militiamen who had never seen cavalry in action before. They broke and ran in the wildest panic while the dragoons followed in hot pursuit, slashing them down or rounding them up as prisoners. Some escaped into the woods.

The flight of the militia exposed the flank of the defenders on the hill, laying them open to a new assault. The deciding blow that drove the Americans from Chatterton's Hill was delivered by a regiment of Hessians. They were commanded by the colonel

whom the British called "the Hessian lion," Johann
Gottlieb Rall.

LIEUTENANT MONROE'S REGIMENT did not take part in
the main engagement at White Plains, but the Virginians were not idle. They managed to surprise and
capture a handful of mercenaries and bring them
triumphantly into camp for closer inspection. Old
Joe Gourd was mightily impressed by one of the cap-
tives who, he said, had "the most infernal set of whisk-
ers I ever beheld."

The prisoners had only recently landed in New
York, and were sent directly to the front—to their
surprise and bewilderment. They had been told they
were only to do garrison duty in America. They were
visibly uneasy in captivity, wondering what would
happen to them. They had been told that the Americans were all barbarians and capable of any atrocity.

The Hessians were mostly tall, husky, and ath-
letic. In full uniform they presented an intimidating
picture, even as prisoners. They wore high, peaked
hats with brass fronting that rose above their heads
like towers. Most of them were tall to begin with, but
the hats made them look like a race of giants. Many
had huge mustaches, which they blackened with the
same polish they used on their boots.

The broad belts that crossed their chests almost
covered their blue tunics. The belts supported their
cartouches, or cartridge boxes, and their bayonets.
Yellow breeches and black gaiters to the knees completed their uniforms. They wore their hair long and

tied in braids that sometimes reached from the nape of the neck to the waist.

There were 30,000 of these formidable creatures fighting on American soil before the war was over, and they caused more hate and bitterness—and death— than any other troops the British sent into the field.

AFTER WHITE PLAINS, it began all over again for the Continentals—retreat. And this time "a most terrible event" came with it.

Lieutenant Monroe and the Third Virginia were among the first troops that Washington withdrew across the Hudson River into New Jersey. But the British were in no hurry to pursue. They had something else in mind first. Sir William Howe faced about and unexpectedly struck his next blow to the south. His objective was nothing less than the strongest bastion the rebels held in America.

Overlooking the Hudson at the northern tip of Manhattan Island stood Fort Washington. Shaped like a pentagon and perched on a rocky bluff 230 feet high, it was intended to deny the use of the river to British shipping. Bristling with cannon and manned by riflemen, the fort was thought to be impregnable. But the British had help when they launched their attack on it. A young officer in a Pennsylvania regiment deserted and made contact with the British. His name was William Demont and he turned over the plans of the fortification to the enemy.

The attack came at dawn on November 16. About eight thousand British troops, including the

Highlanders of the Black Watch, swarmed up the rocky slopes in the face of hot and effective fire from the defenders. Some of the riflemen had to abandon the fight when their weapons became foul and clogged from repeated firing. Resistance was stubborn, but the attack did not waver.

The main assault came from the north and was delivered by battalions of Hessians who pushed doggedly up and forward over the rugged terrain. Taking cover behind the rocks and advancing relentlessly from one boulder to the next, the German mercenaries kept up their pressure on the fort until it could hold out no longer. The final blows were struck by troops under the Hessian lion, Colonel Johann Gottlieb Rall.

It was Colonel Rall who called upon the fort to surrender.

When the defeated Americans filed out of their earthworks to lay down their arms, they had to march between two columns of jeering Germans. Some of the defenders were old men, some were boys of only fifteen, and most of them were so poorly clothed, and looked so little like soldiers, that the British laughed as they slouched past.

The loss of Fort Washington was no laughing matter. It was a staggering blow to American morale. More than 2,800 officers and men were taken prisoner, besides the 53 killed and 96 wounded. Arms, equipment, and precious artillery fell into enemy hands. The Americans had lost their last foothold in New York.

It was George Washington's greatest defeat. No

wonder General Nathanael Greene moaned that the loss left him "mad, vexed, sick, and sorry," as it did Washington himself. "This," said General Greene, "is a most terrible event."

And to the injury inflicted on the American cause, the enemy added insult.

The name of the place was changed from Fort Washington to Fort Knyphausen. This was in honor of Lieutenant General Baron Wilhelm von Knyphausen, the commander of the Hessian forces. And two days later came another disaster: Fort Lee, on the opposite side of the Hudson, was also captured in a surprise assault.

With the forts gone and his army dangerously depleted by casualties and captures, George Washington posted himself in the village of Hackensack, in New Jersey, and took stock. It was a totally depressing prospect he faced. In the year and a half since he had assumed command of the army, he had not had a full day of rest. Now he was, as he wrote to his brother Jack, "wearied almost to death" at the way things were going. He hardly knew which way to turn or what to do. Only one option seemed open to him: to dodge and duck, to play the cat-and-mouse game with the enemy, to keep his army—what was left of it—intact to fight another day. "I have to avoid any attack," he said, "though by so doing, I must leave a very fine country to the ravages of the enemy."

James Monroe was then only a very junior officer, but though he sensed the gravity of the situation he never lost confidence in the cause or its leader.

Years later, looking back, he described how it was then, in mid-November of 1776:

> The enemy, knowing how inconsiderable Washington's forces were, pressed on him, and thus commenced through Jersey a retreat which will be forever celebrated in the annals of our country for the patient suffering, the unshaken firmness, and gallantry of this small band of which the Army consisted—and for the great and good qualities of its commander.

The season was deep into autumn now, and the wind that swept the Jersey plains was turning from biting chill to cold and cruel. No winter clothing had been issued to the troops. What they had been wearing in the summer campaign was worn thin, torn, often in shreds. Toes stuck out of split and gaping shoes. Soles were scuffed paper-thin, or worn away entirely. Feet were lacerated, blistered, calloused. And this was an army continually on the march, always afoot, trudging over unleveled ground that bruised and battered the feet every step of the way.

For the Virginians, unused to the harsh northern climate, the long retreat was a particular affliction. Colonel Weedon—"Old Joe Gourd"—began to fret and worry about his men. He sent back word to Williamsburg that some of them were without shoes and stockings; some without blankets; and almost all without shirts. "The sufferings of my poor men depress me exceedingly," he wrote. "I wish it was over."

It was far from over. Worse was coming.

As Washington's army, or what was left of it, moved west, another army seemed to be on the march in the opposite direction. The roads were clogged with men whose enlistments were up and who were going home regardless of how desperately they were needed. Mingled with the time-expired men were the deserters. "Long Faces," they were called. There were about one hundred of them every day. They were soldiers who simply quit, dropped out, and melted away. Sometimes whole regiments of militia did this, leaving appalling gaps in Washington's troop muster. Once, almost frantic at this steady drain on his manpower, he lamented: "We shall be obliged to detach one half of the army to bring back the other." Sometimes when the men left, their officers went with them. Unable to support themselves and their families on their pay (which seldom reached them), the officers too would decide to let somebody else do the fighting.

All through the war George Washington was plagued by a lack of manpower. Recruiting lagged. Short-term enlistments continually depleted his ranks as release dates fell due. Bounty offers by Congress— ten dollars to anyone who would enlist for three years, twenty dollars and one hundred acres to those who signed "for duration"—did little to help. These difficulties cruelly intensified the plight of the Continental Army as it struggled across New Jersey with the British at its heels.

While Washington marked time in Hackensack, some seven thousand of his best troops were still on the east side—now the wrong side—of the Hudson River. They had been left there under the command of General Charles Lee as a rear guard and to block the possible advance of the British northward. Washington badly needed them now. He sent word to General Lee to bring them over at the earliest possible time.

Nothing happened. Lee did not move.

Washington always treated Lee with great deference, out of respect for his military reputation. But his requests to bring the troops across the river grew more and more urgent: "I must entreat you to hasten your march as much as possible, or your arrival may be too late . . . ."

Still Lee did not move.

Why Charles Lee ignored the appeals of George Washington, and withheld his troops, is not clear to this day. He has been accused of treason on account of it, of deliberately aiding the enemy. (After all, he had been a British officer.) A more generous view is that he actually felt he could do more good by staying where he was and blocking Howe's way into New England. But there is a more likely explanation.

Charles Lee was a vain and ambitious man with an exaggerated idea of his own ability. George Washington had just suffered a series of military disasters and was in a seemingly hopeless situation. Lee probably reasoned that Washington, having shown himself to be incompetent, would resign or be replaced.

By whom?

The answer was obvious: by the man who, as

everyone agreed, was the most able military mind in the Continental army and its most experienced general —Charles Lee.

So General Lee sat tight, waiting to be summoned to take over as commander in chief. Meanwhile, he hardly bothered to hide his contempt for George Washington. "*Entre nous* [among ourselves]," he wrote in a letter at this time, "a certain great man is most damnably deficient." In Lee's opinion, George Washington was "not fit to command a sergeant's guard."

But while General Charles Lee hesitated and delayed, something happened that canceled whatever plans he may have had for assuming command of the army.

He was captured.

In his careless and slovenly way, he often spent the night away from his troops. This time he was staying at the tavern of a Widow White, three miles from his camp. A detachment of British dragoons swooped down on the inn and caught him in the morning before he was dressed. The second-in-command of the Continental Army was ignominiously hauled off as a prisoner of war—unshaven, unwashed, unwigged, and looking generally like a dissipated scarecrow.

The British rejoiced. They had captured the man they regarded as the best American commander, and they fired off guns in celebration. To the rebel cause it was a humiliating blow. Another one.

To many it looked more and more as if there would soon be no such thing as a rebel cause. All that seemed to be left of it was what Colonel Reed called "the wretched remains of a broken army," and that was fleeing before an enemy who threatened to overwhelm and destroy it at any moment.

The broken army was now being pursued by a more formidable and energetic adversary than Howe. Hard on Washington's heels was a general newly arrived from England who could move his troops at twenty miles a day through the rain and over roads ankle-deep in mud. He was Lieutenant General Charles Cornwallis. He had the usual British disdain for the American military, and he vowed he would bag Washington the way a hunter runs a fox to earth. At Newark, Washington's rear guard was just pulling out of town at one side as Cornwallis's vanguard was entering it from the opposite side.

Lieutenant Monroe was there, and he never forgot it. Years later, in a message to Congress, he described the event as a profound experience in his own life. What stayed most vividly in his mind was his first look at George Washington:

> I saw him in my earliest youth, in the retreat through Jersey, at the head of a small band, or rather in its rear, for he was always near the enemy. His countenance and manner made an impression on me which time can never efface. A lieutenant then in the Third Virginia Regiment, I happened to be in the rear guard at Newark, and I counted the force under his command by platoons as it passed me, which amounted to less than 3,000 men.

> A deportment so firm, so dignified, so ex-
> alted, but yet so modest and composed, I have
> never seen in any other person.

The significance of the events he was then living through was not lost on Lieutenant Monroe, either. "The success of the enemy in the battles of Long Island and White Plains," he wrote, "with the capture of Forts Washington and Lee, and the retreat of our army through Jersey, put fairly at issue with the nation this great question: whether they were competent and resolved to support their independence, or would sink under the pressure."

Many on both sides were certain that the cause was surely and steadily sinking under the pressure. Meanwhile, the disasters and near-disasters continued. The narrow escape of the army at Newark was duplicated at New Brunswick where the squeak was even narrower.

At the bridge over the Raritan River there was a duel between the Americans with their long Kentucky rifles and the green-clad *Jägers* with their stubby German pieces. The *Jägers* were so close that their fire caught the Americans tearing up the bridge and drove them off it, but the return fire kept them at bay.

James Monroe and the Virginians were at Brunswick and, along with the other troops, they were ordered to burn whatever tents they still had. There were no carts left to carry the tents and other bulky equipment, so it all had to be destroyed to keep it from falling into the hands of the enemy. The soldiers stood and watched forlornly as the tents went up in flames. The weather was daily getting worse and what little protection they had was being deliberately destroyed.

As the British began filtering into Brunswick, George Washington was completing another letter to Congress asking for help and support. His one-line postscript spoke volumes about the precarious situation of his army. It said: "The enemy are fast advancing, some of 'em in sight now."

Once again the fox escaped the hunters by a hair.

Fortunately, Lord Cornwallis had to rest his men and he suspended his pursuit for four days. It was a hiatus that probably saved the life of the American army. Old Joe Gourd shrewdly assessed the situation in one of the dispatches he was sending home: "The enemy had a mortgage on the rebel army but did not foreclose it."

Now, in December, there were two enemies for the American soldier to contend with and they seemed to be in competition as to which would kill him first—the British or winter.

Winter was the worst. The British themselves were sometimes appalled at the state to which the rebels had been reduced. One of His Majesty's officers took the trouble to examine several American corpses along the Raritan. He was shocked to see that some had no stockings or shoes. Several had no pants—"only linen drawers." There were no proper shirts or vests on the bodies. No blankets were found among the equipment left behind by the rebels. The British officer concluded: "They must suffer extremely."

They did.

In December the enlistment terms of some of the Maryland and New Jersey units expired. They demanded their immediate release. General Hugh Mercer, of the Third Virginia, made them an impassioned speech. He appealed to their patriotism and urged them to stay. He stressed how desperately they were needed, with the enemy scarcely a two-hours' march away. Almost to a man, the militiamen turned on their heels and went home.

George Washington's army, the last and only defenders of the Glorious Cause, had dwindled down to a pathetic 3,400—hardly an army at all. It was nadir, the bottom.

The ragged columns plodded on toward Princeton. There, at least, there was hope of getting out of the cold for a while and sleeping in the college buildings. That would be a blessing. Intrenching tools had long since been discarded. There was no way of digging into the ground anymore to avoid the cutting winds that were sweeping across the Jersey meadows and plains.

There were few, or no, cheers from the people as the Continental columns went slouching along.

The population was often openly hostile to the rebellion. People stopped to scold the soldiers for being so foolish as to fight against the king. Sir William Howe, still the overall British commander, issued a promise of amnesty to all who would lay down their arms and renounce their allegiance to the rebel cause. The proclamation was scattered broadside throughout the state, and hundreds of Americans responded. Loyalists swarmed into the British camps. Defiance to the offer of amnesty was virtually nil. When the Continental Army passed and the British followed behind, Tories broke out their British flags and welcomed the redcoats as liberators.

But the morale of Americans seldom sinks to the vanishing point. Washington's men were not above enlivening things with a spot of plunder, with Tory houses the special targets. Particularly the cellars of Tory houses. At Brunswick some soldiers found a generous cache of liquor in the home of a rich Loyalist and for a while the retreat became more of a stagger than a march.

"They got a disorder which at camp is called Barrel Fever," one officer noted. "It differs in its effects from any other fever—its concomitants are black eyes and bloody noses." So there was some horseplay and high spirits along the way.

And though there was more than enough gloom and despair to go around, the inborn American optimism proved to be unquenchable. "Never was finer lads at retreat than we are," boasted Samuel Webb, a Connecticut officer. "About 2,000 of us have been obliged to run damn'd hard before about 10,000 of the enemy. No fun for us that I can see. However, I cannot but think we shall drub the dogs. . . . Never mind, all will come right one of these days."

At Princeton the commander in chief himself

found it necessary to stay with his rear guard and
supervise the felling of trees that were set across the
road to impede the British advance. He saw personally
to the destruction of bridges.

Lieutenant Monroe also did duty at Princeton
where five Virginia regiments were stationed to cover
the retreat of the rest of the army into Trenton. When
troops, stores, and baggage were concentrated in that
town on the Delaware, the Virginians joined them.

Now the Continental Army, what there was of
it, huddled on the banks of the river that had been
George Washington's objective all through the retreat. He wished to put the river between his army
and the British, using it as a moat, a barrier. There
would be a respite on the other side, another breathing
spell, where his bone-tired soldiers could rest for a
while. And where he himself, "wearied almost to
death," could catch his breath.

What would happen after that? He had no idea.

As RIVERS of the nation run, the Delaware is not impressive. It is swift enough, but narrow, rambling,
and winding. For the soldiers from Virginia, including the commander in chief, it compared unfavorably
with the Potomac, which was broader and deeper. The
memory of the Hudson was fresh in the minds of
most of the troops, and here the comparison was even
less to the advantage of the Delaware. All along the
route of retreat there had been rivers to cross—the
Hackensack, the Passaic, the Raritan. This one appeared to be just more of the same.

Baggage and supplies went across the river first. Boats and rafts took them from the Jersey side to the opposite shore in Pennsylvania. Then came the troops, some of them barely able to stand. They shuffled on the boats and rafts while some of the townspeople stood on the dock and laughed at what somebody called this "apology for an army."

The loading and crossing went on all day long and into the night. One observer of the scene looked upon it with a trained and sensitive eye, and he never forgot it. He was the painter Charles Willson Peale, who was then a lieutenant in Washington's army. He had raised his own company of eighty-one men, and clothed and fed them himself. He was wearing a black cocked hat with a gold button in the front of it, and a gold loop around it. He carried a rifle with a primitive telescopic sight on it.

Darkness fell. Fires blazed along the river. Long lines of shadowy figures wavered toward the boats in the flickering light. Hour after hour they came, as the artist watched—the gaunt veterans of Boston and New York and of three weeks of retreat across New Jersey. Now and then a cannon was tugged forward inch by inch to the grunts and curses of ghosts. Now and then —a rare spectacle—a creaking cart with its emaciated horse.

"The most hellish scene I ever beheld," said Charles Willson Peale. "The watch fires fanned by an icy wind and dancing in reflection on the river . . . Distorted, leaping shadows everywhere . . . Hurry . . . Confusion . . . The imminent presence of danger

... The long shouts and the wild, bawling execrations of the men ..."

The artist shrank back when one of the ghostly figures stepped out of line and approached him. The man was quivering and his teeth chattered. He had lost all his clothes. "He was in an old, dirty blanket jacket, his beard long, and his face so full of sores he could not clean it." Only when the man spoke to him did Charles Willson Peale realize, with a terrible shock, that this creature was his own dear brother James—"Jemmy!"

It was daylight of December 8 when the last boat left the Jersey shore. And almost immediately the British came marching into the town, with bands playing and flags flying, hot on the heels of the departing Americans. Some of the boats were still in midstream when the enemy appeared. Cannonballs from artillery on the far side arched over the departing Continentals in the river and landed among the arriving British.

Had Lord Cornwallis arrived a few hours earlier, he might have caught the exhausted Americans with their backs against the river and helpless against a charge by the oncoming Hessians and Highlanders.

The Continental Army would almost certainly have been wiped out then and there, on the east bank of the Delaware. But the bridges that had been destroyed, and the tree trunks that had blocked the roads, and the incurable British habit of moving too late, had saved the American cause again.

Cornwallis did not give up at the water's edge. He marched his troops to a place called Coryell's

Ferry fifteen miles above Trenton. His intention was to cross immediately and overtake the Americans on the other side. But there was not a boat or raft to be had. George Washington had taken the precaution of seizing every single craft up and down seventy miles of the river. The British were immobilized on the Jersey shore.

It did not cause them much concern. They were sure the campaign was over for the winter anyway. The beaten and decimated Americans could be disposed of at leisure later. The main body of the British were sent back to New York City. A string of outposts and strong points were set up along the river. Lord Cornwallis, convinced that everything had been tidied up and battened down for the next few months, packed up for a holiday in London. In the spring he would return and sweep up the remnants of the rebel army, and the war—if you could call it a war —would be over.

Great numbers of Americans thought so, too.

In New York City a group of prominent citizens issued a document in opposition to Tom Jefferson's Declaration of Independence. It was a "Declaration of *D*ependence." In it these citizens—Loyalists all— proclaimed their continued allegiance to the king. They supported "the Constitutional Supremacy of Great Britain over the Colonies." They called for a speedy restoration of the union of America with the mother country. This union, they said, was "the unfailing source of their mutual happiness and prosperity."

The Declaration concluded by calling the war "the most unnatural, unprovoked Rebellion that ever disgraced the annals of Time . . ." It was signed by more than seven hundred Loyalists. All during December similar petitions were circulating, and none of them ever lacked for signatures.

With public support for the Revolution dissolving day by day; with his army melting away like snow in springtime; with nothing in prospect but more defeat and retreat—it was no wonder that as 1776 neared its end, George Washington was privately saying:

"I think the game is pretty near up."

V

THE DAY OF GLORY

JAMES MONROE once said that he was not "fonder of the inconveniences that attend the active part of the army than most people." He had no more liking for what he called "the usual fatigue and danger" of a campaign than anyone else. Still, he was one of those who made the Revolution possible by serving gladly and steadily. His sturdy confidence in the cause was what sustained him. And although it isn't every junior lieutenant who attracts the attention of generals, James Monroe had a way of catching the eye of his superiors.

One of the best commanders in the Continental Army, Brigadier General William Alexander, took the young officer from the Northern Neck under his wing. Alexander styled himself "Lord Stirling" and was customarily addressed as "Your Lordship." This was based on his claim to a hereditary Scottish title which the House of Lords had refused to validate but which the American insisted he was entitled to anyway.

General Alexander was no less an American patriot for claiming to be a British nobleman, and he went out of his way to advance the military career of

109

James Monroe. But on the west bank of the Delaware, in the winter of 1776, the future of the American army and everyone in it seemed perilously dim.

Few of the rebel regiments had reached the river with as many as 200 men left. Most were down to 90, and some as low as 40. Monroe's own regiment numbered only about 160 enlisted men, with something like 450 sick or on furlough or otherwise absent. The officers were similiarly depleted. He was one of the few still fit for duty, and his value to his superiors increased accordingly.

Lieutenant Monroe was quartered in the Thompson-Neely House, part of which was given over to a hospital for sick soldiers of whom there were many. The long strain of the march, the insufficient food and inadequate clothing, made the men easy prey to disease and infection. Dysentery and pneumonia and fevers raged through the ranks. The deadly typhus spread from camp to camp. Smallpox was epidemic.

There were two other military hospitals in nearby towns and their floors were covered from wall to wall with the sick and dying, who had no other place to lie down. Sometimes four or five men would die on the same straw before it was changed. There were no nurses, no soap, and no sanitation facilities. The stench was intolerable. Army hospitals in the Revolution were far more hazardous to the life of the soldiers than the battlefield ever was.

Medical care was primitive when it was not barbarous, and there were never enough doctors or medicine. Bandages were scarce and usually filthy, with blood poisoning as the common result. There was no anesthetic for amputations, which were frequent with the inevitable onset of gangrene. When a leg or an arm was sawed off, the victim was simply given a glass of rum to dull his agony or a bullet to bite on to suppress his screams.

As December wore on and the weather worsened, the proportion of men on the sick list reached the appalling figure of six out of every ten. And those who were technically fit for duty were almost as wretched as the ill. Clothes that had served through the summer were now, in the dead of winter, in tatters. The hunting shirts of the riflemen hung on them in shreds and were infested with vermin after their months of use with no change or laundering. But a buggy shirt was better protection than nothing at all, and nothing at all was what many of the soldiers had. To make things as galling as possible, the British were snug in comfortable quarters on the other side of the river and well aware of how badly things were going for the Americans. The British commander, now a major general named Grant, sent word to Colonel Johann Gottlieb Rall, the commander of the garrison at Trenton: "The enemy have neither shoes nor stockings, are in fact almost naked, dying of cold, without blankets and very ill supplied with Provisions."

It was the coldest December anybody could remember. The army was reduced to sending men into the countryside begging for old clothes. Washington himself wrote thank-you notes when they came in. One batch of 113 blankets was turned in by a group of patriotic citizens—who charged the army cash for every one of them. The bill came to £678 12*s*. 6*d*. This included the cost of cleaning. The charge for the blankets was a crushing burden on the army and on the government, since the national treasury was virtually bankrupt.

The contribution of the Continental Congress in Philadelphia to these difficulties was to call for another day of "solemn fasting and humiliation" because of the distressing state of the American cause. This was on December 11. The next day Congress fled to Baltimore for fear the British might seize Philadelphia at any moment. Before departing with its quills and papers and inkpots, the Congress turned over its powers to George Washington, making him the virtual dictator of America. Some began calling him the "Lord Protector."

It was a grandiose title, but his power resided solely in the pitiful scraps and leftovers of a fighting force that had once proudly called itself the Continental Army. Now it was, as somebody said, "crouching in the bushes," strung out thinly along twenty-five miles of river. Weak and exhausted everywhere, it showed no signs of recovery or potential anywhere. Surveying his woebegone troops, weighing their condition, looking to the immediate future, George Washington made a judgment: "Ten days more will put an end to the existence of this army."

Ten days...

THE BAD NEWS spread rapidly, as it always does,

through all the thirteen states, which now seemed in danger of becoming colonies again. Revolutionary zeal, which had always fluctuated and flickered, all but evaporated from New Hampshire in the north to Georgia in the south. There was always a hard core of patriots who never wavered, but in the winter of 1776 even so stout a supporter of the cause as Elkanah Watson of Plymouth, Massachusetts, gave up hope. "We looked upon the contest as near its close," he wrote afterwards. "We considered ourselves a vanquished people."

Among soldiers and civilians alike, morale was never lower. "A thick cloud of darkness covered the land," said an American officer. "Despair was seen in almost every countenance."

When and how George Washington decided on the move that changed the course of the war, and saved the Revolution, is not known. On December 14 he wrote a letter to Governor Jonathan Trumbull of Massachusetts, which showed that something was brewing in his mind. He spoke of attempting "a stroke on the forces of the enemy" who, he said, were scattered and not expecting an attack. "A lucky blow in this quarter would be fatal to them," he wrote, "and would most certainly raise the Spirits of the People, which are quite sunk by our late misfortunes."

Before he could make a move of any kind, he had to have more men. He sent officers all over the state to round up recruits. Congress, before running away, sent him a battalion of Germans raised in Pennsylvania and Maryland. Fighting on the patriot side, they would in a measure offset the effect of their countrymen, the hated Hessians.

During a heavy snowstorm Major General John Sullivan came riding into camp at the head of the troops whom Charles Lee had been so hesitant about delivering to Washington. They were greeted with shouts and cheers but they were a sorry lot—"much out of sorts and in want of everything." Their number had been reduced to a mere two thousand by desertions and expired enlistments, but they helped.

Major General Horatio Gates also turned up with five hundred men, mostly New Englanders. The muster rolls lengthened, but many of the newcomers were unfit, and most of them were destitute of supplies and equipment.

Still, when mid-December had come and gone, Washington had more men he could call upon for active duty than when he crossed the river. And these were the best men of all: hardened troopers, most of them—soldiers who had been through the mill and who had not been broken in the grinding.

The situation on the other side of the river was of first importance to Washington as he brooded over his next move. Where were the enemy's units located? Were they making preparations to cross the Delaware and attack? If so, when and how? To find out, George Washington made every effort to procure spies he could rely on.

He found some, often paying them out of his own pocket. They filtered information to him on the deployment of British troops and their movements.

One of his most successful agents, according to local tradition, was known as John Honeyman. He was a butcher and cattle dealer by trade. Today that would be described as his "cover." It allowed him to circulate freely among the British who dealt with him to supply meat for their troops. John Honeyman learned much that was of vital interest to George Washington.

While sending military intelligence to the rebels Honeyman also pretended to be a spy for the British, thus acting as a double agent. One day American scouts, thinking Honeyman was working for the enemy, captured him and delivered him bound hand and foot to Washington's headquarters. Washington was closeted with the alleged Tory for an hour or more, supposedly interrogating him as an enemy spy. Then Honeyman was ordered locked into the guard-house for the night, with a trial—and probable hanging—scheduled for the following day.

That night John Honeyman escaped and re-newed contact with the British connections. He reported that the rebel army was in far too wretched a state to be of any concern. Nothing was to be feared from it. The British command could put its mind at ease and relax for the winter, said John Honeyman.

His escape had no doubt been arranged by Washington, who also briefed him on the misleading intelligence he was to take back across the river. But more important than what Washington's agents were telling the British was what his spies were telling him.

He learned that the enemy was sprinkled along a line of outposts—Bordentown, Trenton, Princeton,

Brunswick, Amboy. The English troops were stationed farthest from the river. On the Delaware itself, at Trenton and Bordentown, were the Hessians.

George Washington studied the dots on his map and he said: "Now is the time to clip their wings while they are so spread."

All that remained was to pick the right place and time to strike. That would have to be decided soon. The river would not remain a barrier for long. An intercepted letter revealed that the British command was waiting for the river to freeze over before launching an attack across it that would carry the redcoat army all the way to Philadelphia. The river had frozen solid many times in previous winters. It could happen again, at any hour, with a sudden drop in temperature.

Washington would have to act, and soon.

By night the lamps and candles burned late in the Keith House, on the side of Jericho Mountain, where George Washington was quartered. Outside in the snow, the sentry paced up and down along the stone wall in front of the house. In the fields beyond, half-naked soldiers shivered around their campfires, some of them sleeping on the frozen ground with their feet to the flames. Across the dark river the lights of Trenton flickered dimly, reminding everyone that the enemy was there, waiting. Inside the house, night after night, there was a council of war.

The fate of unborn millions—the phrase was George Washington's—now depended on the decisions of the men around the long table on the first floor. Washington would sit in his high-backed chair facing the fire. Lord Stirling, who suffered from a painful stiffness that was either rheumatism or arthritis, sat with his back to it, absorbing its heat. The other officers were grouped around the table or stood leaning against the wall as they listened. At a table to one side sat Captain Alexander Hamilton, taking notes. At the far end of the room, seated on a chest perhaps, Lieutenant Monroe might be paying respectful attention but offering no comment of his own. It was honor enough that, as the favorite of Lord Stirling, he was there at all.

The pressure on Washington increased not only from day to day but from hour to hour. He had to reckon with a possible attack by the enemy across the frozen river, "the bridge of ice," but he also had to face the possibility that soon he might have no army at all. Or not enough of one to count. This was because the enlistments of whole units would be running out by January 1, and now December was fast nearing its end.

"Even a failure cannot be more fatal than to remain in our present situation," was the argument pressed on Washington by his adjutant, Colonel Joseph Reed. If Jersey, or even some part of it, could be retaken—why, said Colonel Reed, "the effects would be greater than if we had never left it." He had a concrete proposal. Why not, he asked, a stab of some sort "at or around Trenton"?

Washington's own intent had been running in the same direction. On December 23, 1776, he put his decision into writing for the first time in response to

Colonel Reed. The date for the attack on Trenton would be "Christmas Day at night, one hour before day."

This was a top secret communication. "For Heaven's sake, keep this to yourself," Washington pleaded. "The discovery of it may prove fatal to us..."

The younger officers knew that something big was in the offing and they were intensely eager for it to happen, whatever it might be. With other men of Lord Stirling's brigade, Lieutenant Monroe had been scouting along the river and doing guard duty at fords where the enemy might attempt to cross. Patrols were sometimes sent over the river by night to feel out the terrain and reconnoiter the enemy's positions. James Monroe was sent on these forays as well. He was doing in deadly earnest on the Delaware what he had often done in boyhood play on the Rappahanock and the Potomac.

Quartered in the same house with Lieutenant Monroe was another young officer, whose hearty and outgoing personality was in strong contrast to James's customary reserve. William Washington, a distant relative of the general, was twenty-four years old and a captain. He had been wounded in action and his flair for leadership had won him rapid promotion and the respect of everyone. Few who came in contact with this brawny and boisterous Virginian suspected that he had been studying for the ministry when he joined the Continental army.

Icy gusts were blowing in from the river on De-

cember 23 when the beat of the drums summoned
the soldiers to form up by regiments for an unusual
ceremony, on orders of General Washington. At the
head of each regiment, an officer began reading to the
troops from a pamphlet. It was Tom Paine's newest
trumpet-call in print, and it was called *The Crisis*. The
officers had to raise their voices to a bellow to be heard
above the wind, but the men caught the words and
they ran through the ranks like a flame:

> "These are the times that try men's souls . . .
> He that stands now deserves the thanks of man
> and woman. . . . If there was ever a just war since
> the world began, it is this in which America is
> now engaged. . . . We fight not to enslave, but to
> set a country free, and to make room upon the
> earth for honest men to live in."

The effect of Tom Paine's words was to kindle
a fire inside the soldiers that went far to ward off the
cold of hopelessness and defeat.

ACROSS THE RIVER, in the little town of Trenton with
its one hundred houses, Colonel Johann Gottlieb Rall
paraded his troops every day.

The colonel was proud of his regiment. He never
failed to attend the daily changing of the guard at
2:00 P.M. Standing musket-stiff before the large frame
house on King Street that was his headquarters, he
savored the spectacle no matter how many times he
saw it.

His grenadiers wore the dark blue uniform, and two hundred of them marched past when the guard was being changed. Stepping smartly, they swung their heads eyes-right in perfect unison as they passed the colonel. The daily parade always included two of the brigade's cannon and the brigade band. This was what Colonel Rall enjoyed most. He had a passion for military music. His junior officers sometimes complained that he seemed to care more about having the band instruments kept in immaculate order than about the condition of the grenadiers' muskets. Besides the music, the colonel was fond of drink. Off duty he was a convivial fellow, always ready for a bout of tippling or an all-night binge.

His British superiors were a little uneasy about giving Johann Rall command of a post as critical and important as Trenton. Trenton was the linchpin that held their extended line on the east side of the Delaware together. It was the hinge of all their Jersey defenses. Besides being headstrong and rather erratic in his behavior, the Hessian colonel could not read or write English. All orders and other communications from British headquarters had to be translated for him.

Still, when it came to fighting, his achievements were formidable. He was not called the Hessian lion for nothing. During an attack Johann Rall could always be found where the action was hottest and the bullets thickest. He had distinguished himself at the battles of Long Island and White Plains. And in the capture of Fort Washington he had added to the legends of Hessian valor and élan.

He himself regarded his Trenton command as no more than his due. If anything, he thought the post hardly equal to his abilities. His attitude was conditioned by his contempt for the Continental Army and his scorn for the American soldier. Several times he was cautioned that though there was a river between him and the enemy, Trenton was not impregnable. Fellow officers repeatedly pointed out to him that it would make military sense to throw up redoubts and earthworks around the town as a precaution. Colonel Rall scoffed at the idea. He had every confidence in the three crack regiments that made up his brigade, about 1600 men in all.

Colonel Rall's attitude toward the Americans and the possibility of an attack was expressed when he said: *"Lasst sie nur kommen! Keine Schanzen! Mit dem Bajonet wollen wir an sie!"*—"Just let them come! We don't need any earthworks or trenches! We'll go at them with the bayonet!"

Tory agents and deserters informed him repeatedly that, on the other side of the Delaware, the Americans seemed to be preparing to move. The colonel dismissed that as "old woman's talk," and he brushed off another warning with "Nonsense! These country clowns cannot whip us."

AT ONE of his war councils, George Washington had posed the question on which everything else depended: could his army be gotten across the turbulent river, at night, in the dead of winter?

The commander in chief directed his question at

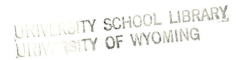

a stocky bantam of a man with red hair and an aggressive look. He was Colonel John Glover, the commander of the Fourteenth Continental Regiment.
Washington, and everybody else in the council, knew
how much hung on John Glover's answer. If he said
no, the hoped-for blow could not be delivered. The
situation then would, in truth, be hopeless—for the
army and for the cause.

The answer came quietly and without bluster.
"Your Excellency," said John Glover, "it can be
done. And my boys will do it."

The relief around the table was like something
tangible in the air. Everyone was confident that if
John Glover said it could be done, it *would* be done.
The war might have ended months ago on Long
Island if Glover's regiment had not saved the beaten
army and its equipment by ferrying them across the
East River in a morning fog.

No other unit was equipped to do what the Fourteenth could do. It was made up mostly of sailors
from Marblehead, Massachusetts. They marched and
fought as infantry, but their natural element was the
water. They were expert with both oars and muskets.
The men from Marblehead were Washington's spe-
cialists in amphibious warfare.

Being sea-going, the Fourteenth had wider hori-
zons than most of the other regiments. Negroes sailed
in the fishing fleets, and there were blacks in John
Glover's regiment. Though George Washington had
been against enlisting blacks at the beginning of the

war, his attitude changed. Black soldiers fought on the American side in almost every great action of the Revolution, beginning with Bunker Hill and continuing to the end at Yorktown. There were blacks on the Delaware among John Glover's sailormen.

On the morning of December 24, the patriot Dr. Benjamin Rush visited Washington at his headquarters and found him busy with papers on his desk. One of them fell to the floor and the Doctor picked it up. He noticed three words that Washington had written on it. They were *Victory or Death*.

The general did not explain the words, but *Victory or Death* was the countersign he had chosen for the attack on Trenton. The phrase expressed the extremity of the gamble he was taking: he made no allowance for failure or retreat.

The attempt to seize Trenton was extremely bold, but it was not reckless. It was not sheer, crazy desperation. Washington and his staff had worked out a plan of attack in which surprise would be the decisive element. A three-pronged crossing would carry the rebel forces over the river. This would be followed by a pincer movement that would lock the town in a clamp and capture it.

George Washington himself would command the main force of Continentals, which would land on the other side about nine miles above Trenton. General James Ewing would take another column over, closer to the town and behind it, to cut off any Hessian retreat. Colonel John Cadwalader would cross with his troops, mostly militia, further downstream to distract the attention of the enemy garrison at Bordentown and keep it from reinforcing Trenton. It was sound militarily, but it involved precise timing and the coordinated movement of separated columns marching under their own commands at night. George Washington wrote out his general orders for the assault: "General Stephen's brigade to form the advance party . . . The brigades of Mercer and Lord Stirling, under the command of Major General Greene, to support Gen. Stephen . . . Four pieces of artillery to march at the head of each column . . ."

Now the sluggish and shivering camp stirred to life, and a general bustle replaced the customary apathy. Cooks and their helpers fanned up their fires to prepare the three-day rations that the general ordered. "Firecakes" were baked on hot stones out of soggy dough, and whatever meat was available was thrown into the iron kettles. As also ordered by the general, the camp was combed for blankets which were then issued to the troops that would make the crossing. Each man was given forty rounds of ammunition. If the attack should exceed expectations the men would be supplied to push on and take advantage of any favorable development. The enterprise had a grasping-at-straws atmosphere about it, but it was well organized.

Orders went out for doctors and their aides to report from the outlying military hospitals. Medical men were also sought from the surrounding countryside. Should the assault on Trenton turn out to be a disaster, casualties would be heavy. The appeal for doctors brought little response.

All day on the twenty-fourth the general rode up and down the river bank inspecting the preparations, checking on the distribution of powder and ball, and on the number of cannon that would be available. There weren't many. He was, as always, grave and unsmiling as he sat tall on his horse, but his look of cool confidence never varied. It was like a reassuring slap on the back for the soldiers who would, next day, follow him to Trenton.

Lieutenant Monroe was making his own preparations and seeing to those of his men. He and the other Virginians were proud that their own generals had been chosen by Washington to lead the assault, as announced in the General Orders.

But the orders also contained a paragraph that had far more personal impact on James Monroe than the assignment of the Virginia generals. The paragraph read: "Captain Washington . . . with a party of forty men . . . to march before the divisions and post themselves on the road about three miles from Trenton, and make prisoners of all going or coming out of the town."

Captain Washington immediately began assembling the forty picked men he would need for his mission, but a difficulty quickly became apparent. Sickness and malnutrition had so ravaged the manpower of the officers corps that no lieutenant in Captain Washington's company was fit for duty. When this was reported to Colonel Weedon, he issued a call for volunteers.

JAMES MONROE was as eager for glory and advancement as any young officer. The "enthusiastic zeal" with which he had joined the army had not lessened, despite the months of discouragement and defeat he had lived through since leaving Williamsburg. He was the first to respond to Colonel Weedon's appeal.

So when it came time to cross the Delaware, Lieutenant Monroe was no longer with his home unit, the Third Virginia. Instead, he was second in command to his new friend William Washington on the hazardous mission called for in the general orders.

Christmas Day broke cold and bleak along the Delaware. The troops collected their gear, rolled their blankets, checked their flints, stuffed their rations in their haversacks, and prepared to march. Nobody thought of stopping to celebrate the holiday. That was left to the Germans across the river. They were known to be sentimental about *Weihnacthen,* marking it with much feasting and drinking. Let them . . .

The river boats that Washington had rounded up to keep from the British were now brought out of their hiding places. They had been concealed in creeks and inlets, and behind heavily wooded Malta Island several miles upstream. There they were invisible to the enemy on the other side. Skilled river men brought them down, some twenty-five of them, to a place called McKonkey's Ferry,[1] where Washington's column would cross.

In all, his force did not total more than 2,400 men but that number, meager as it was, included his most reliable units, the elite of what was left of the Continental Army. They were the leather-tough campaigners that Nathanael Greene, ex-blacksmith and fighting Quaker, was talking about when he said: "We bear beating very well . . . the more we are beat the better we grow."

At about 2:00 P.M. they began forming up and marching out of their camps toward the river. They were to assemble on Wrights Town Road, "one mile back of McKonkey's Ferry." The wind had shifted to the northeast, a bad sign, and as they neared the river a light snow began blowing in their faces.

Captain Washington had been chosen for the special mission because his courage and leadership had been noticed by his superiors. He, in turn, had promptly accepted Lieutenant Monroe as his second in command. Monroe had shown soldierly spirit by volunteering, and Captain Washington had come to value him as a reliable comrade besides. He was physically strong and agile, and he was not likely to be easily rattled.

At McKonkey's Ferry, James Monroe and his detachment came upon a scene of confusion bordering on turmoil. Soldiers were milling about, seemingly

1. Located at what is now Washington Crossing National Park, Bucks County, Pennsylvania.

without plan or purpose. Orders were being shouted into blasts of winter wind that carried them away unheard. Riders came galloping with dispatches for the officers inside the Ferry Inn who were working out the last details of the crossing. The excitement generated by the tumult and hubbub was contagious, and Monroe and his men were infected with it as they awaited further orders. Far from brooding over the hazards that lay ahead, they were tingling for the action to begin.

Old Sam McKonkey, a salty local character, seemed to have taken charge of the proceedings. He was an enthusiastic patriot, proud that his inn had become the focal point of so important an operation of the Continental Army. Officers and men alike were fond of Sam McKonkey. He sold his rum readily for Continental money while other merchants of the area refused to accept rebel currency for anything. Old Man McKonkey would have liked to cross with the troops, and they would have been glad to take him along.

On the river bank the bellow of a mighty voice was making itself heard above the howl of the rising wind. Colonel Henry Knox's lung capacity was equal to his heft, which came to 280 pounds. He had no need of loudspeaker, public address system, or megaphone. Those who experienced his voice at full blast usually described it as "stentorian." He needed all the decibles he could produce as he boomed his orders to the straining and gasping artillerymen who were dragging his precious guns toward the waiting boats.

The colonel was struggling like a maniac to wrestle his guns across the Delaware River from the Pennsylvania side to the Jersey. There were only eighteen of them left. And General Washington, from his temporary headquarters in McKonkey's Inn, was supervising the loading of his shabby little force for the crossing which, as he well knew, would be crucial to his career and to his cause. The omens were not good, and as night came and wore on they got worse.

There were, of course, no war correspondents on the river to take down notes and then describe the scene for the newspapers later. But we know how it was. We know from letters and diaries and descriptions, some of them as vivid and detailed as the best modern correspondents could produce. Henry Knox himself wrote one such letter after Trenton, to his wife. One of Washington's officers kept a diary, with entries like:

> Christmas, 6 P.M.— . . . It is fearfully cold and raw and a snowstorm is setting in. The wind is northeast and beats in the faces of the men. It will be a terrible night for the soldiers who have no shoes. Some of them have tied old rags around their feet; others are barefoot, but I have not heard a man complain. They are ready to suffer any hardship and die rather than give up their liberty . . .

Another of Washington's officers reported an unforgettable detail of the drama: Major James Wilkinson had been to Philadelphia and was returning to the Delaware camp on Christmas Day. He had no difficulty finding his way to where the troops were assembling. "Their route," he said, "was easily traced, as there was a little snow on the ground, which was tinged here and there with blood from the feet of the men who wore broken shoes."

Major Wilkinson had dispatches to deliver to Washington. The general, whip in hand, was about to mount his horse when Wilkinson found him. The interruption was unwelcome. "What a time is this to hand me letters!" the general growled.

The young major, abashed by the difficulty he was causing, explained that he had been ordered to deliver the papers by General Gates.

"By General Gates?" Washington was surprised. "Where is he?"

It developed that Horatio Gates was on his way to Congress—in Baltimore.

"To Congress!" Washington echoed, dumbfounded.

It was disturbing news. Horatio Gates was one of the experienced officers on whom Washington depended. Now, when he was most needed, he was gone. He had evidently lost confidence in the success of the crossing and was detaching himself from the whole enterprise. His visit to Congress also had disagreeable possibilities. Horatio Gates was quite capable of intriguing against the commander in chief behind his back.

Washington looked grim as he stuffed the letter

into a pocket, mounted, and rode off to the river bank without another word.

When the sun went down, the first troops were herded to the edge of the river toward the waiting boats, which were a reassuring element in a highly dubious and uncertain venture. Each one was like an enormous canoe, but solid and seaworthy. Some were sixty feet long. They were named after the Durham Iron Works and were designed to take iron ore, produce, and merchandise up and down the Delaware. They could be poled upstream and rowed downstream with eighteen-foot sweeps.

Fully loaded, the largest Durhams could carry an entire regiment—men, equipment, cannon, and even horses. They were pointed at either end and usually painted black. They only drew some twenty-four inches of water, so the men could wade ashore from them on the other side. Only George Washington's foresight in gathering up all the Durhams on the river and keeping them in readiness until needed made the crossing possible at all.

In the first of the boats to cross the Delaware that night was Lieutenant Monroe and the forty men of his special detachment. Like the others, he cringed and shivered when the arctic gusts of the open river swept across the open Durham as it pushed into midstream. His fringed hunting shirt, once so smart and trim, was now torn and shoddy, and gave him scant protection. The hat that had been so jauntily cocked in sunny Virginia was now a sodden lump on his head. The only thing that distinguished it at all was a piece of white paper pinned to it so that the men could spot him in the dark as an officer. All the officers wore bits of paper on their hats that night.

The men themselves, most of them, were hunched in soaked and threadbare blankets, which gave even the most intrepid warriors among them the look of miserable old women. They crouched low in their seats, trying to use the gunwales as protection against the savage wind that howled across the water. James Monroe never forgot those harrowing moments in the dark on the Delaware as his tossing Durham headed for the hostile Jersey shore. But he had a curious lapse of memory when, years later, he recalled the crossing.

A half-century later he wrote about the event with his usual restraint, playing down his own role. His detachment, he said, "passed the Delaware in front of the army, in the dusk of the evening, at Coryell's Ferry, 10 miles above Trenton." This is almost certainly an error. No other account speaks of a crossing at Coryell's Ferry, and everything that happened to James Monroe on the other side indicates that he crossed at McKonkey's Ferry with the others.

He remembered vividly what happened when he landed on the Jersey side, alone with his little troop in enemy territory:

"After crossing the river I was sent with my command [a piece of artillery] to the intersection of Pennytown [now Pennington] and Maiden Head [now Lawrenceville] roads, with strict orders to let no one pass until I was ordered forward. Whilst occupying this position, the resident of a dwelling some distance up a lane had his attention directed to some unusual commotion by the barking of dogs. He came out in the dark to learn the cause, and encountered my command, and supposing we were from the British camp ordered us off.

"He was violent and determined in his manner, and very profane, and wanted to know what we were doing there on such a stormy night. I advised him to go to his home and be quiet, or I would arrest him. When he discovered that we were American soldiers, he insisted that we should go to his house and not stay out in the storm, and he would give us something to eat. I told him my orders were strict and we could not leave. When he returned to the house, he brought us some victuals.

"He said to me, 'I know something is to be done, and I am going with you. I am a doctor, and I may help some poor fellow.' When orders came for us to hasten to Trenton, the doctor went with us."

The orders to hasten on did not come for many a tense hour.

The moon was well up when the main body of George Washington's column began climbing into the Durhams, regretting the campfires they were leaving and unhappy about the uncertainties they were facing. They stiffened in their seats as they felt the boats settle lower and lower into the water with the added weight of newcomers. The tension always increased

when, at a bellow from Henry Knox, the fully loaded
boat shoved off from the solidity of the dock into the
turbulence of the roaring river.

As the tattered troops kept coming through the
dark in long, shadowy lines, they had nothing of the
smartness of parade-ground soldiers about them. They
looked, rather, like a procession of scarecrows that
had spookily come to life. But there was spirit and
purpose in those wavering files as they wound their
way to the river. One witness, watching them in the
light of the winter moon, was thrilled to the core at
the sight. To young Captain Hamilton, waiting his
turn on the river bank with his cannon, the men—
"every devil of them"—looked "ready to storm hell's
battlements in the night."

With the first units across the river, George
Washington had reason to think that his operation
might still proceed according to plan, despite the de-
parture of Gates and the worsening weather. But dispatch riders brought reports that warned him that his
grand design was crumbling at the edges. Colonel
Cadwalader was having difficulties lower down on the
river, and he needed encouragement. Washington
scribbled off a hurried message: "If you can do nothing real, at least create as great a diversion as possible."
Even in so disturbing a situation Washington, always
the gentleman, signed his note according to the polite
usage of the time: "Yr. most ob^t Servt"—Your Most
Obedient Servant.

It developed that Cadwalader actually got some
of his men over the river that night. But, once there,

he decided that floating his cannon and horses across that stormy current would be impossible. So he returned to the safety of the Pennsylvania side. He assumed that Washington would not be able to get across, either.

General Ewing, who was to land his troops south of Trenton and cut off the enemy's retreat, was even less enterprising. He marched his men to the river, took a long look, and decided that such a stream on such a night was impassable. General James Ewing promptly marched his men back to camp. He reported later: ". . . the Quantity of Ice was so Great." Long before that historic night was out, the projected three-pronged thrust across the Delaware River had dwindled to one slender column—George Washington's weatherbeaten Continentals, and only 2,400 of them.

He was not yet aware of the collapse of the two supports he was relying on when the main body of his army began moving across the river at McKonkey's Ferry. But the knowledge of the twin disasters downstream would not have deterred him. "I have never seen Washington so determined as he is now," said one of the officers who was with him that night.

The first full unit across was the Virginians under General Adam Stephen, as specified in the general orders. The Durhams were packed solid, with the gunwales only inches above the water.

The early contingents got across without much difficulty. At this point the Delaware River was only about 700 feet wide, not much more than the length of two football fields. But the weather deteriorated with dismaying speed, and the river itself grew increasingly hazardous as the crossings went on. On the preceding days it had been comparatively free of ice. But far upstream, at the beginning of the week, there had been a spell of intense cold that froze the river solid. Now it was midweek, and a thaw had loosened the upstream ice. It came coursing down the river on the swift current in huge chunks and solid blocks that were sometimes six inches thick. Every one was like a jagged rock that had somehow learned to float. They slammed against the sides of the wooden Durhams like missiles fired from guns.

All the grit and skill of the brawny Marblehead seamen was needed to get the boats across. The sailors grunted and cursed as they manned the poles and sweeps that moved the tossing Durhams from shore to shore. They had only the most precarious footing on the narrow, icy decks and could be pitched into the roaring river at any moment. Others, with other poles, had to fend off the crashing slabs of ice that threatened to stave in the sides of every boat every foot of the way.

Everything worsened when, at about eleven o'clock, the snow turned to sleet, which the wind drove into the faces of the men like the slashing of knives. In their rags and tatters they were worse than naked; the wet cloth froze stiff against their skin and rubbed it raw whenever they moved. And there was no relief when the voyage ended. They had to wade ashore up to their knees through water that was crusted with ice and chilled the marrow numb in their legs. Once on solid ground, there was nothing to do but stand helplessly in the open while the storm continued to beat upon them without mercy. For hours.

When enough men were across to assure that a bridgehead had been established and that others would follow, George Washington crossed, too. His immediate staff and about forty enlisted men made the passage with him in one of the smaller Durhams. The mood was grim. The officers were depressed, most of them sure that the expedition was already doomed by the worsening weather, if nothing else. The enlisted men lapsed into glum silence.

Washington had to squeeze himself into a smallish space next to Colonel Knox, whose more than ample width took up more than his share of the seat. Everybody in the boat was electrified by the reaction of the commander in chief to this situation. He growled out a coarse but funny comment about the size of the colonel's behind, urging him to shift his big fat arse with care, otherwise it would tip the boat over and drown everybody. The jest was so unexpected, coming from the commander at such a time, that the entire boat came to life with laughter and a spurt of warmth ran through the soaked and shivering soldiers. George Washington's joke on the Delaware about Henry Knox's massive buttocks became a legend in the Continental Army.

There was no joking on the other side.

Washington wrapped his cloak around him and

sat down on an unused beehive, which became his command post as he supervised the arrival of the rest of his troops. It was a weary business, and it went much more slowly than he had anticipated. Glover's sailormen worked with unflagging energy and skill, but the driving sleet had iced everything over, making every step and movement uncertain and dangerous. Horses slipped and reared, not only causing delays but menacing life and limb for their handlers. Ferrying the cannon, and especially the heavy howitzers, proved almost impossibly difficult as they, too, became coated with ice and froze first to the ground and then to the boats. But, as Henry Knox remarked, "perseverance accomplished what at first seemed impossible."

Washington and his staff had hoped to have all the men, guns, and horses across the river by midnight. But it was three o'clock in the morning of December 26 before the last two artillery pieces were deposited safely on the Jersey shore, along with ninety cannonballs and four horses. The Marblehead sailors had brought George Washington's army across the Delaware River by night and by storm, as promised, without losing a man, a gun, or a horse, but the operation was three hours behind schedule. And another hour went by before the march on Trenton could begin.

General Stephen's men had formed a protective arc out from shore, and now the regiments had to be formed up within it and gotten into proper marching order. Washington rode among the troops, inspecting the various units, offering encouragement, giving advice: "Soldiers, keep by your officers! For God's sake, keep by your officers!" Once, as he rode up an icy bank, his horse's hind feet slipped out from under him, and for an awful moment it looked as if the beast would go down and crush his rider under him. But Washington, a superb rider, seized the horse's mane and the animal righted itself.

It was about 4:00 A.M. when the march began, and Trenton was still nine miles away. There would by daylight at about seven o'clock.

Nothing in Washington's bearing indicated that he had lost hope of catching the enemy off guard by swooping down on the town before sunup, but he had grave misgivings as the column began to move. He had gambled everything on the element of surprise, but time had run out. "This," he wrote later, "made me despair of surprising the town, as I knew well we could not reach it before the day was fairly broke. But as I was certain there was no making retreat without being discovered and harrassed when repassing the river, I determined to push on at all events."

Some of the firmness of the leader passed into the column and a renewed spirit spread through the ranks as the long, deadening wait ended and the march began. The snow on the ground softened the tread of the regiments as they plodded forward, and it muffled the rumble of the guns on their creaking carriages. The "profound silence" that the commander ordered was almost literally achieved.

Late as it was, Washington was still anxious to

preserve as much of the element of surprise as possible. This made the mission of Lieutenant Monroe's detachment doubly important. Isolated at its lonely station, and remote from the main body of the army, the detachment saw to it that nobody passed down the road to Trenton with warning of the approaching attack. There was, in spite of the storm, some traffic on the roads that night. As Monroe later reported, a number of citizens were unceremoniously seized on their way to and from the town. They were held as prisoners of war.

But there were long, empty waits between these flurries of activity and, as all soldiers know, waiting can be the most nerve-racking ordeal of all. Alone in the storm and dark, with no word of how the operation was progressing—or even if it *was* progressing—the detachment's vigil became a test of stamina and resolution. Hour after hour, the men could only stamp their feet and hug themselves for warmth, and pray that they wouldn't be left stranded while the decisive action of the night passed them by.

The column, meanwhile, was now well on the road, slipping and lurching as it plodded blindly through the night. The snowstorm had thickened, making the dark more impenetrable than ever, and the ice was torture on unshod feet and toes wrapped only in rags. To save the men from total exhaustion, a halt was called about midway in the march at a place called Birmingham, a crossroads. Here the men broke out their rations and gnawed on the cold meat from their haversacks and munched on their tasteless firecakes. Washington himself ate as hastily as the others, without even dismounting from his horse.

While they were resting, one of the officers expressed a worry that was bothering many in the column, officers and men alike. Captain John Mott, who was acting as guide for the column, called attention to the fact that his priming powder was damp in spite of his attempts to protect it by covering it with his handkerchief. His weapon was a fusee, a short, light musket, but the difficulty would apply to all the weapons. If the weather prevented the guns from being fired, how could the soldiers be expected to fight a battle?

It was a desperate situation and the problem was passed up the chain of command to George Washington himself. It did not faze him for a moment. His answer was: "Use the bayonet and penetrate the town. The town must be taken!" Without further orders, the men fixed their bayonets.

At the Birmingham crossroads Washington split his little army into two divisions. Major General John Sullivan was given command of the right wing, which included Glover's Marblehead regiment, among other troops, and nine artillery pieces. He was to take the lower, or river, road which roughly followed the line of the Delaware to Trenton.

The left wing was commanded by Major General Nathanael Greene who also had nine guns and about half the troops, including the Virginians under Adam Stephen and Lord Stirling. This column was to take the upper, or Pennington, road, which was a little longer than the lower route. General Sullivan, accordingly, was to make a short delay in his march so that the two columns would reach Trenton at the same time. The assault was to be delievered simultaneously from two sides.

Washington had all officers set their watches with his before the command to march was given. He himself elected to ride with General Greene's column on the Pennington road. The command "Shoulder your firelocks!" was given, and the columns moved off.

Not all the soldiers marched at the first command. Two of them would never march again. Many had fallen asleep at the roadside, despite the snow and sleet. Officers had to circulate among them and shake them awake. Two privates did not respond to the shaking and shouting. They had frozen to death.

Farther along the Pennington road, Lieutenant Monroe and his detachment were still guarding the crossway and wondering when, and if, they would ever be relieved of their isolated vigil. The hours of separation and uncertainty seemed endless, and the night was almost gone before their ordeal was over.

A dim and ghostly dawn was just beginning to break when the first of General Greene's advance scouts became faintly visible in the murky half-light as they approached the crossroads. A surge of excitement and relief went through the men of the detachment. They had not been abandoned or forgotten after all. The attack on Trenton was still on, and they would be a part of it.

Captain Washington's command, its mission accomplished, was absorbed into the main column. Lieutenant Monroe took his place in the vanguard, not far behind the scouts. The doctor who had joined him just after the landing was still with him. The doctor's name, he said, was Riker. Nobody ever learned what his first name was . . .

The march went through thickets of black oak and hickory and past farmhouses that were silent and dark. Now the driving snow and sleet were on the backs of the troops, instead of in their faces, which was a relief. Many of the men covered the firing pans of their muskets and rifles with their clothing or blankets. Some held their weapons with the firing pans tucked into their armpits. As the soldiers stumbled and slipped through the night, their officers spoke to them in low tones, urging them to ready themselves to revenge the disasters of Long Island and the Hudson forts. The password *Victory or Death!* ran through the ranks.

With Trenton still two miles away, the column came to an unexpected stop. A small body of men was spotted in a lane at one side of the road ahead. To everyone's amazement, they turned out to be Americans. What on earth were they doing there?

George Washington rode up to find out.

The men turned out to be members of General Stephen's brigade. Their leader was Captain Richard Anderson, of the Fifth Virginia Regiment. He explained that he had been ordered across the river the day before by General Stephen to reconnoiter. He and his men had had a brief fire-fight with some Hessians, and wounded several of them. The rest had withdrawn.

Washington was furious.

This blundering raiding party had no doubt stirred up a hornet's nest in Trenton and alerted every soldier in the town. The commander turned on General Stephen, who sat mounted at his side. How dared he dispatch soldiers across the river without orders or authorization? "You, Sir," Washington growled, "may have ruined all my plans by putting them on guard!"

But he had only consideration for the men themselves. He knew they must be exhausted after their long prowl in enemy territory. He had them join the head of the column instead of tiring them further by ordering them to the rear.

But the episode must have been dismaying to the commander. Bit by bit, he had seen his carefully conceived plan crumble away, with its absolutely essential element of surprise evaporating into nothing as the night wore on. It was getting to be broad daylight. How could his approach to Trenton be concealed? And now this senseless raid had surely wiped out the last possible chance of taking the Hessians unawares.

The commander was not to be deterred. "Press on, boys!" he ordered. "Press on!"

ON CHRISTMAS DAY in Trenton there had been excitement and alarm when the American reconnaissance party struck. The day, a Wednesday, had not been a holiday for the troops on duty. Of the three Hessian units in the town, Colonel Johann Rall's was the "regiment of the day" and so was under arms and responsible for the safety of the garrison. That morning there had been the ceremonial changing of the guard, as usual, together with the routine details of any other day. At nightfall the troops on duty had turned in at the "alarm houses" in the lower end of town where they slept fully clothed. The regiment of the day always did this in case of attack. Guns were stacked in front of the alarm houses, in instant readiness.

For the troops not on duty—the Lossberg and Knyphausen regiments—a certain amount of celebrating was permitted. *Weihnachten*, Christmas, was more of an occasion for Germans than for Americans. There was more eating and drinking, and more conviviality, than on a normal day. The celebration included decorating the *Tannenbaum*, the Christmas tree, a custom that was new to America. The holiday spirit was prevalent, but there was no rampant revelry or widespread intoxication with soldiers reeling bleary-eyed through the streets.

At about eight o'clock, as everyone was preparing to relax for the night, the shots of a fire-fight were heard. Instantly the town was in an uproar. The day before, a warning had come from British headquarters in Princeton that the Americans were planning some kind of an attack on Trenton.

This must be it.

The Rall regiment was immediately turned out to meet the emergency. The shots had come from the outskirts of town to the northwest where the farthest of the Hessian pickets were posted on the Pennington road. The American patrol had opened fire on the outpost, wounded six of the pickets, and driven the rest back to the town. Then the invaders had melted away into the woods.

A search by the first Hessian officers on the scene proved fruitless. When the Rall regiment hurried to the scene, there were no Americans to be found.

Colonel Johann Rall himself came cantering up to survey the situation. Mindful of the British warning, he wished to see the extent of the supposed American attack and to counteract it if necessary. When nothing further developed, the colonel wheeled his horse about and rode back to town. He was annoyed. He had been having an agreeable game of checkers at his headquarters with a local resident named Stacy Potts, and he did not relish being called out on Christmas night, and in such wretched weather, for no good reason.

One of his officers suggested that it would be wise to send patrols out on all the roads, and especially to the ferry approaches. Fortunately, Colonel Rall's reaction to these perfectly sound proposals was typical of him. He repeated his opinion that the Americans were "a miserable band" and "a bunch of farmers." Tomorrow would be soon enough to take any necessary precautions. For now, the threat was over. Forget it.

So, in a way that neither George Washington or anybody else could have foreseen, the unauthorized foray of Captain Anderson and his men turned out to be an invaluable stroke for the patriot cause. Though it temporarily alerted the enemy, it had the further effect of being mistaken for the thrust that the British had warned against. Since the attack, such as it was, had come to nothing, Colonel Rall concluded that the danger was over. He called off the alert.

The troops went back to quarters. They were happy to get indoors and enjoy the coziness of a fireplace and share in whatever food and drink was still available to cap off Christmas Day. The colonel himself was also pleasure bent. He did not return to headquarters to finish his checker game with Stacy Potts. He found livelier amusement instead.

There was a party going on at the house of Abraham Hunt, who was Trenton's most prominent citizen and a Tory. The Hunts set a lavish table—venison, and turkey, and roast goose, and plenty of hot buttered rum. All this was much to the taste of Johann Rall, and he entered into the festivities with gusto. The party went on all night; and when an unwelcome interruption came, the colonel did not allow it to spoil his fun for long.

A local Tory, a farmer, had urgent news for Colonel Rall. Not being able to deliver his message at the colonel's headquarters, the Tory had traced him to Abraham Hunt's house. There a servant barred his way at the door. The merriment was too well under way for the servant to allow an unknown farmer to burst in and interrupt it. The Tory then scribbled a note, folded it over, and insisted that the servant deliver it to Colonel Rall at once. This the servant agreed to do.

The colonel was deep in a card game with a fragrant tankard of hot rum at his elbow when the servant ventured to approach him and hand over the note. Johann Rall scarcely glanced up from his cards and his rum. He took the note and, without reading it, stuck it into his coat pocket.

What the message said was that an American army was, at that very moment, marching on Trenton.

It was about eight o'clock of the morning after Christmas, December 26, 1776. The snow and sleet seemed to be increasing when guides informed George Washington that his column was less than a mile from Trenton. One of the guides was David Lanning, a blacksmith who lived in the neighborhood. A sturdy patriot, he had been captured by the Hessians several days before but managed to escape with the help of the same Stacy Potts who sometimes played checkers with Colonel Rall. Passing himself off as a woodchopper, and carrying an axe for disguise, Lanning had gotten through the enemy lines and offered his service to Washington.

With Lanning's warning that the goal was so near, word was passed down the column and the pace of the march began to quicken. Lanning pointed out a large shack up ahead on the Pennington road. Washington recognized it as the shop of a cooper—a maker of barrels and casks—which his spies had told him was used as an outpost by the Hessians. The column was getting close to its target.

Just as the advance skirmishers emerged from a woods and into a clearing, Lieutenant Andreas Wiederhold of the Knyphausen Regiment stepped out of the shack. He was the commander of the outpost, and for a moment he was confused by the unexpected appearance of what he thought was a stray party of Americans. But he soon raised the alarm, and the Hessian pickets came tumbling from their shelter to hoarse cries of: *"Der Feind! Der Feind! Heraus! Heraus!"* —"The enemy! The enemy! Turn out! Turn out!"

The Americans kept advancing, firing three times as they came. Lieutenant Wiederhold cooly waited until they were closer before giving his own command to retaliate. Then an answering volley was delivered. It had no effect.

The patriots were now swarming out of the woods in numbers that the picket post had no hope of stopping. The Hessians began to fall back on the town. They withdrew in good order, not in panic. Washington, at the head of his troops as always, took note of the enemy's conduct under fire and had good words for them afterwards. "They behaved very well," he said, "keeping up a constant retreating fire . . ."

Now the town of Trenton was plainly in sight, all one hundred houses of it, in broad daylight. George Washington waved his sword and shouted to his men: "There, my brave fellows, are the enemies of your country. Remember now what you are about to fight for!"

Despite the slip and slide of the icy footing, the whole column surged forward at a "long trot"—on the double—or, as Colonel Knox reported: "We entered the town pell-mell." And there, miraculously, in spite of the long delay, in spite of the broad daylight, in spite of everything, the surprise of the assault was almost complete. The weather, which had been the enemy of the expedition from the start, had become its salvation for it had kept the normal Hessian patrols indoors.

The Americans came storming into Trenton unopposed. The smashing surprise of the assault was the greatest element in its final success. Given no chance to organize the formations in which they had been trained to fight, the Hessians were at a disadvantage from which they never recovered.

HAVING BEEN among the first to cross the Delaware, Lieutenant James Monroe was now among the first to charge into Trenton. Old Joe Gourd's Third Virginia was the spearhead of the attack, and Lieutenant Monroe was in the vanguard of the regiment, side by side with Captain Washington. As they surged forward, they could hear shooting on the other side of the town, the river side. General Sullivan's column had arrived and, with perfect timing, begun its assault at the same moment that Washington's column struck.

The sudden attack from both sides shocked and

rattled the Hessians further. The confusion of the defenders deepened as the patriots came charging at them—"with great spirit"—from everywhere. The shouting, yelling attackers must have looked like specters from another world to the astonished mercenaries. Ragged, gaunt—some barefooted, many nearly naked, most in mud and tatters—they spread panic and terror by the wildness of their appearance and the intensity of their attack. The Hessians were trained to face any troops on earth that came at them in traditional order of battle, and in conventional style, as proper soldiers should—but this!

This was more like an Indian raid, with muskets, rifles, and bayonets taking the place of tomahawks, arrows, and knives.

The two main streets of the town were King (now Warren) and Queen (now Broad). They ran roughly north and south and converged at the northern end. It was at this point that the Virginians, led by William Washington and James Monroe, burst into town.

Both the invaders and the defenders knew that much depended on which side could control King Street. At the other end of it the Hessians were bringing up artillery to block the Americans from advancing deeper into the town. Their weapons here were two brass three-pounders, which could do devastating damage to oncoming infantry.

Each of the guns was drawn by four horses, and there was much bellowing and lashing by the gunners as the animals plunged in their traces, straining to haul the cannon into position without a moment's delay. It took an officer and eight men to serve each piece. In the comparatively narrow span of the street, the guns, their crews, and the horses built a formidable barrier across the main avenue of the American advance. The cannon and the cannoneers came under American fire at once.

Riflemen posted behind the fence of a nearby tanyard began sharpshooting at the Hessian gunners. Patriot artillery was wheeled up and was soon booming its shells toward the enemy battery. Lieutenant Monroe and his men, stationed in the *V* where King and Queen streets came together, sent splatters of hot lead whistling toward the enemy.

Several of the gunners were dropped in their tracks, but the cannon kept firing. Three of the four horses on one of the cannon, and two on the other were hit. Still the three-pound shells kept belching from the brass muzzles of the Hessian guns. At times the solid shot was varied with grapeshot, which sprayed deadly iron pellets in all directions. The Hessian stand on King Street was doing more to block the American advance than any other resistance that the enemy was able to offer.

The guns would have to be silenced.

Captain Washington and Lieutenant Monroe put their heads together and reached an instant decision. Quickly they told their men their plan. It was as simple as it was bold: capture the cannon.

With shouts of encouragement to their men, the young captain and the younger lieutenant led the headlong rush of the Virginians straight at the Hessian artillery. The enemy gunners had called for support from their infantry, and now the menace of musketry was added to the terror of cannon shot as the Americans pounded forward through the snow and slush. But with the wind blowing sleet into the eyes of the defenders, none of the musket balls found a mark, and not a man was felled by cannon shot.

The American riflemen paused only once in their charge. At a command from their leaders, they halted, sank down on one knee, took careful aim, and sent a withering volley at the Hessians. Then they stormed up to the cannon, where only four defenders were left at one of the guns and six at the other. The Hessians who hadn't already run for their lives were overwhelmed and taken captive. The guns were put out of action and left for further use by American artillerymen. The main barrier to the American advance was broken.

In describing the action long afterward, James Monroe spoke of it with a modesty that few military heroes have ever matched. "Capt. Washington," he said, "rushed forward, attacked, and put the troops around the cannon to flight, and took possession of them." There was no mention by James Monroe of Lieutenant Monroe in this account of the episode, even though Lieutenant Monroe was in the forefront of the charge, shoulder to shoulder with his captain.

The capture of the two Hessian cannon was, in fact, a turning point of the Battle of Trenton. The clearing of the upper end of King Street permitted

George Washington to complete a maneuver that led to the entrapment and surrender of hundreds of the defenders. Later the general said that in every other action he had seen, there was always some misbehavior by some of his soldiers; but at Trenton *everybody* behaved well. And no act of individual bravery had more bearing on the outcome of the battle than the wild charge against the Hessian cannon on King Street, with Lieutenant James Monroe in the lead.

The Virginans did not stop there.

Scarcely pausing for breath, they pressed on and drove the defenders back before them. As they pushed eastward toward an area where a concentration of the enemy was being threatened with encirclement, they came under heavy musket fire. There Captain Washington was hit twice in quick succession. He was led from the field, badly wounded in both his hands.

What happened then was described by James Monroe in his cool and detached way:

"The command devolved on Lieut. Monroe, who advanced in like manner at the head of the corps, and was shot down by a musket ball, which passed through his breast and shoulder. He also was carried from the field . . ."

Three of his soldiers carried him to a room in a nearby house that had been commandeered as a field hospital. His wound was a bad one. The musket ball, in tearing through the chest and shoulder, had severed an artery. Blood spurted from the wound.

"I would have bled to death," Monroe said afterwards, "if this doctor had not been near and promptly taken up the artery."

The doughty Dr. Riker had accompanied Lieutenant Monroe and his unit not only along the whole march through that tempestuous night but right into the thick of the street fighing. And his prediction at the start that he might be able to help "some poor fellow" in case of trouble came true: the poor fellow turned out to be Lieutenant Monroe himself. Had the ruptured artery not been "taken up," or surgically closed, at once, the future fifth president of the United States would have perished, at the age of eighteen, in a pool of blood on a slushy street in Trenton, New Jersey.

Monroe, barely conscious and in great pain, was treated in the same room where William Washington's wounds were also being tended. Dr. John Cochran, the future surgeon general of the Continental Army, was also in attendance in that primitive and improvised field hospital. Between the two dedicated doctors, Lieutenant Monroe's wound was dressed and treated with as much skill and professional knowledge as the medicine of the time and place could provide.

But the Hessian musket ball remained in his body for the rest of his life . . .

OUTSIDE, the battle was turning into the kind of combat at which the Americans excelled—the frontier style of fighting that had inflicted such damage on the British at Concord. The storm was still blowing, but many of the men had somehow contrived to keep their powder and firing pans dry, and their flints as well. Enough muskets and rifles were in working order to sting the Hessians repeatedly and from all sides.

The Americans fired at close range, and with deadly effect, from behind fences and trees, from house windows and cellars, from side streets and alleyways. Afterwards the Hessians complained that the rain and sleet prevented them from bringing their own weapons into play while the Americans, hidden and dry in the houses, picked them off at will. Now the storm was beating into the faces of the defenders, blurring visibility and adding to their confusion and distress.

The village became a place of indescribable turmoil, tumult, and chaos. Something like four thousand men were teeming and raging through its narrow streets—shooting and shouting; slashing at each other with bayonets; screaming in pain and staining the icy slush with their blood. The veil of falling snow was dirtied by the haze of gunpowder, and an unnatural darkness-by-day gave the mad melee an eerie and unreal atmosphere. The civilian residents of the town huddled in terror in their houses, some of which caught fire and began to burn around them.

The American cannon kept pace with the rifles and muskets. From a high spot overlooking King Street, the guns of Captain Hamilton boomed menace and defiance to everything within range. The gunners had found ways to protect the touchholes of their pieces from the wet; round shot and canister went whistling down the streets of Trenton, making the Hessians run for their lives. When they sought to flee the town to the eastward, Major Glover's amphibious Marbleheaders blocked their way with raking fire from well-placed batteries which they served as readily as they handled boats.

"Our cannon dispersed them and the fight became a chase," said a Virginia officer. "When ordered to pursue the enemy, we stepped off with alacrity, in full cry." The Virginians were by no means the only ones in the chase. The troops of Colonel John Stark, all New Hampshire men, did noble work with musket and bayonet, driving the Knyphausen Regiment before them as they advanced through the town. The Pennsylvania German Battalion was deployed to block the retreat of the Hessians toward Princeton, a mission it carried out with spirit and success. It was German against German in the Battle of Trenton.

Once, weeks before, after a minor American foray across the river, Colonel Johann Gottlieb Rall said he welcomed such excursions by the enemy. Perhaps, he said, George Washington himself might be foolhardy enough to try the same thing. Then he, Johann Gottlieb Rall, would have the pleasure of taking the American commander prisoner. But when George Washington actually did appear in Trenton, Colonel Rall missed his chance by a wide margin.

He was in bed, fast asleep, when the Americans burst into the town. The all-night Christmas party, and his copious intake of rum, left him dead to the world when the great crisis of his military career

broke upon him. A young lieutenant, who had heard
the firing of the approaching Americans, came pounding on his door. It took quite a lot of racket to get the
colonel out of bed and on his feet. Finally, still in his
nightshirt, he appeared at his bedroom window and
was heard asking blearily: "What's the matter? What
is it?" He soon found out, and it was enough to clear
his head and galvanize him into action.

Colonel Rall was quickly dressed, soon down-
stairs, and in another moment on his horse. He was a
stupid and arrogant man but a brave soldier, and he
ordered a counterattack. He was determined to get
the town back in his possession. He attempted to organize a charge of his own regiment supported by the
Lossberg Regiment, with the Knyphausen units in reserve. The brigade band struck up the music he loved
—drums beating madly, pipes squealing—and Colonel
Rall bellowed the command: "Forward, men, forward!"

King Street was to be the line of advance, but
not many of his troops followed Colonel Rall's lead.
The cannons of Capain Alexander Hamilton dominated the area, and American musket and rifle fire
cut into the Hessian ranks with murderous effect. A
captain standing not far from his commander was
hit, and fell dead in the street. A younger officer was
hit in the leg and hobbled off, useless for further
combat. Another lieutenant was struck in the spine
and fell to the ground. The bayonets of the Hessians,
on which Colonel Rall was accustomed to rely, were
useless against a foe who could not be reached or even

seen. Before the Hessian column could get under way, it was hit by Hugh Mercer's Virginians on the left. The counterattack disintegrated before it was properly launched.

Then Colonel Johann Gottlieb Rall, the proud professional who had held the "country clowns" in such contempt, ordered a retreat—and the command had hardly been given when he was hit twice in the side, and fell from his horse. Two of his soldiers picked him up and led him away to the Methodist church, which was near, and there he lay in agony. Later he was taken to his own headquarters, where he died. The story has it that when he was being undressed, the note that had been delivered to him at the Christmas party fell out of his pocket. Somebody read it to him. Said Colonel Rall: "If I had read this at Mr. Hunt's I would not be here."

Leaderless now, attacked from every side, beaten wherever they met the enemy, the Hessians were seized by a single idea: to get away. Already a detachment of British dragoons, who were part of the garrison, had mounted their horses and galloped off to Princeton and safety without firing a shot. The Hessians tried to take the same route to the rear, but it was too late. Many of them were hampered by the mounds of plunder they had accumulated and were unwilling to leave behind. Their overstuffed packs and overloaded wagons slowed their flight and made them easy prey to the pursuing Americans.

One way out of Trenton went across a stream called Assunpink Creek, and some Hessians got across it by wading through the icy waters up to their necks. Some scurried across the bridge. But not many. Whichever way the Hessians turned in their panic and flight they found Americans—infantry or cannon or both—blocking their way. The town was enveloped. There was no way out.

Milling helplessly around the Assunpink Bridge, with American cannonballs falling among them, the remains of the Knyphausen Regiment gave up. The commanding officer, Major Friedrich Ludwig von Dechow, had been badly wounded in the hip. He came limping to the American lines, accompanied by a corporal. The corporal was holding up a spontoon, a kind of pike or spear that officers sometimes carried. On it was tied a white handkerchief.

In an apple orchard on the eastern edge of the town, the Rall and Lossberg regiments were huddled together in the last stage of disintegration. A half-moon of American troops blocked the way to the Pennington road. Gaping at them with lethal menace were the muzzles of six cannons commanded by Captain Thomas Forest. The position was hopeless.

There were some attempts at negotiation, with the Hessian officers talking to the Americans through interpreters. But, in the end, the only answer from the American side was: "Surrender immediately, or we'll blow you to pieces."

One by one, the Hessian standards were lowered.

The Hessian officers put their hats on the tips of their swords and held them up as a sign of submission.

Some Hessian soldiers laid their weapons on the ground at their feet. Others were so outraged at what was happening that they smashed their gun stocks against the nearest tree, cut the straps of their cartridge pouches, or simply hurled their weapons into the woods.

General Lord Stirling, as the senior officer in the American advance, rode forward and received the swords of the Hessian officers.

And then the whole village seemed to explode to the shouts of the American soldiers. They threw their hats in the air, those who had them. They hugged and kissed each other and danced wild jigs in a kind of delirium. They rolled in the slush and mud of the Trenton streets in sheer exuberance. The unbelievable had happened, and *they* had made it happen.

They had taken sweet and overwhelming revenge on a detested enemy who had humiliated them, laughed at them, and repeatedly beaten and killed them. They had gotten their own back for Long Island, and Kip's Bay, and the Hudson forts, and the long ordeal of the Jersey retreat. They had, in fact, done more than they knew. They had saved the Revolution.

George Washington knew it.

He was riding down King Street, tall and conspicuous on his big, reddish-brown horse, when an officer came galloping up as fast as the ice underfoot allowed. It was Major Wilkinson with the news that the last of the Hessian units had thrown down their arms.

James Wilkinson was a young man, and he never
forgot what happened then. The commander leaned
over in his saddle, took his hand, and pressed it
warmly. His face was beaming.

"Major Wilkinson," said George Washington,
"this is a glorious day for our country!"

FOR SIZE and scope and casualties, Trenton cannot
compare with the great battles of history. Not a single
American soldier was killed in the fighting, which
lasted hardly more than an hour. Only about twenty-
five Hessians lost their lives. But no other victory has
meant more to American history, and very few battles
in all history have had the lasting significance of
Trenton.

Historians have since outdone each other in describing the significance of Washington's crossing of
the Delaware. It "struck the blow which decided the
issue of the war," according to John Quincy Adams.
Another historian goes further and calls the crossing,
and the victories that followed, "the campaign that
changed the history of the world."

When word reached London, there was con-
sternation and dismay. "All our hopes were blasted by
that unhappy affair at Trenton," moaned Lord
George Germain, the secretary of state for American
colonies. And a British traveler in America named
Nicholas Cresswell was astounded at the psychological
impact of the American victory. "The minds of the
people are much altered," he wrote in his journal. "A
few days before they had given up their cause for lost.

Their late successes have turned the scale and now they are all liberty mad again. . . ."

A cause that had been given up as lost came surging back to life. The glorious madness for liberty revived. The Revolution, which had been tottering on the brink of final collapse, pulled back its shoulders, threw out its chest, and went striding forward again toward the goals that the great Declaration had set forth.

There were plenty of disasters ahead. Philadelphia would be taken by the enemy. The troops would starve and freeze at Valley Forge. They would mutiny at Morristown. The South would become a battleground. Charleston and Savannah would fall. Men would desert.

But after the Delaware, the country never again came so close to utter despair. The cause was never again so close to extinction. Because Trenton was won, the Revolution was won.

WITHDRAWING from Trenton turned out to be almost as agonizing as getting there. The weather was still intolerable. The river was just as dangerous as before. The men were near total exhaustion. Some of them were reeling drunk from tapping forty hogshead of rum found in the town. They were in no condition to continue the campaign. The tireless Marblehead sailors brought them back across the river.

With them went nine hundred Hessian prisoners, six captured cannon, one thousand weapons, forty horses, wagonloads of baggage, twelve drums, and fifteen battle flags. So many prisoners, so much booty, so complete a victory amazed military men all over the world. Sir William Howe, for one, was staggered. He could not believe that "three old-established regiments of a people who make a profession of war should lay down their arms to a ragged and undisciplined militia."

But more shock and surprise was immediately in store for Sir William and for Lord Cornwallis, whose trip home had been rudely interrupted by the patriot victory. He hurried to Princeton and, with eight thousand men, marched on to Trenton. Washington, back across the river again, was there to meet—and outmaneuver—him.

Cornwallis did not arrive until nightfall and decided, in the familiar British way, to postpone his attack until morning. Washington left his campfires burning all night, but he swung his army around Cornwallis's left and rear, and then marched swiftly to Princeton, ten miles away. At daylight he swooped down on three British regiments, which had no idea he was anywhere near, and routed them completely. It was a victory as dazzling as Trenton.

As the British went tumbling off in all directions, George Washington was heard to shout to his men: "It's a fine fox chase, my boys!" The humiliating fox-hunting bugle on Harlem Heights was fully revenged.

After Trenton and Princeton, Sir William withdrew to lick his wounds. Not a single one of his soldiers was left in New Jersey, which so recently had been under his full control. Washington's astonishing twin victories moved even the Prussian war lord

Frederick the Great to express admiration: "The achievement of Washington and his little band of compatriots between the twenty-fifth of December and the fourth of January, a space of ten days, were the most brilliant of any recorded in military annals."

George Washington was not above making a display of his triumphs. He knew it would be good for morale—soldier and civilian alike. And, being human, he did not object to a public flourish that would offset the spreading criticism of him as an incompetent general. There had been enough reports of failure and defeat. Let there now be a display of victory.

The captured Hessians were paraded through the streets of Philadelphia, with the captured battle flags and booty behind them. All the patriots of the town turned out to watch the spectacle and cheer. Here were the hated Hessians, thought to be invincible, reduced to the lowly status of prisoners. Look—

> ... the Hessian band
> That dared invade fair freedom's land

—had been thoroughly bested by our own fellows, shoeless and shirtless though they might be! The hope and pride of the patriots soared. The assurance of the Tories sank and, in many cases, evaporated. One of the spectators noted that the Hessians—"all fine, hearty men and well clad"—looked more fit than their guards, who were "mostly in light summer dress, and some without shoes." The guards, however, were "stepping light and cheerful."

The prisoners were in charge of Colonel George Weedon—Old Joe Gourd—of the Third Virginia. That of course, was Lieutenant James Monroe's regiment, but he was not there to join in the parade, or even see it.

As the most seriously wounded of all the American soldiers at Trenton, he had been taken back across the Delaware. He had missed the surrender at Trenton, and the rejoicing over it. He had been lucky to come away with his life. Hurt, sick, exhausted, and not always conscious, Lieutenant James Monroe was *hors de combat*, out of action, a casualty of war.

But if he missed the victory parade, he could afford to.

He had had his hour of glory.

VI

AFTERWARDS

FIFTY YEARS LATER, as President of the United States, the names of those who had saved his life and restored his health on the Delaware were still in his mind—the doctor who closed his wound and the Pennsylvania family named Coryell who nursed him through the early stages of his recovery. He never found a descendent of Dr. Riker whom he could reward with a public office, but he never forgot him.

It was, after all, James Monroe's record as a soldier that launched him on the career that ended in the White House. After Trenton, he went on to serve at Brandywine and Germantown, at Valley Forge and Monmouth. When the war was over, the people of Virginia, impressed by his qualities as both soldier and man, sent him first to their House of Delegates and then to the Continental Congress.

And when the time came, the same qualities that made James Monroe a good soldier made him a solid President. Those qualities were character and courage, and a passion to serve his country. His friend and mentor Thomas Jefferson summed him up in one vivid sentence: "Turn his soul wrong side outwards and there is not a speck on it."

Monroe did not become one of America's greatest presidents, but he left his country bigger, stronger, and more prosperous than he found it. He fixed his place in history with his Monroe Doctrine, which closed North America to future colonization by European powers.

He was a public servant for forty-seven years, and almost every major office and honor in the gift of the American people came his way. But at the end, what he remembered most proudly was the tribute he won in his youth, on the Delaware. It had come from General George Washington himself, and it read:

> I take occasion to express the high opinion I have of his worth. The zeal he discovered by entering the service at an early period, the character he supported in his regiment, and the manner in which he distinguished himself at Trenton, where he received a wound, induced me to appoint him to a captaincy....
>
> He has in every instance maintained the reputation of a brave, active, and sensible officer.

And that essentially described the entire career of James Monroe, not only as soldier but also as statesman and citizen. He was, always, a brave, active, and sensible American.